Leading Healthy, Biblical Small Groups

A Guide for Small Group Leaders

Leading Healthy, Biblical Small Groups: A Guide for Small Group Leaders
© 2025 Kent Shepherd. All rights reserved.

Published by Shepherd Ministry Resources
Steens, Mississippi

Paperback ISBN: 979-8-9931843-1-9

First Edition — October 2025
Printed in the United States of America

Cover design: Kent Shepherd (with assistance from KDP)
Interior charts/graphics: Kent Shepherd (with assistance from Gemini)

Unless otherwise indicated, Scripture quotations are from the ESV® Bible (The Holy Bible, English Standard Version®), © 2001 by Crossway, a publishing ministry of Good News Publishers. ESV® Text Edition: 2016. Used by permission. All rights reserved.

Dedication

To my brother in Christ, **Jerry Lavender.**

Your love for small groups and your faithful example of service have inspired me more than words can express. Whether it was making sure there were enough chairs, gathering materials, brewing the coffee, or simply being present to meet the needs of others, you consistently demonstrated what it means to be a true servant of Christ.

Thank you for modeling a heart that quietly, yet powerfully, points others to Jesus. Your example has reminded me—and so many others—that leadership begins with service, just as our Lord taught: *"But whoever would be great among you must be your servant"* (Matthew 20:26, ESV).

This book is dedicated to you, my friend and fellow laborer in the gospel.

Contents

Dedication iv

Preface vii

Introduction: Why Small Groups Matter ix

Part 1: Foundations 15

Chapter 1: The Biblical Foundation of Small Groups 16

Chapter 2: The Character of the Small Group Leader 32

Chapter 3: The Framework of Small Group Ministry 47

Part 2: Principles 65

Chapter 4: Preparation 66

Chapter 5: Presentation 82

Chapter 6: Participation 100

Chapter 7: Prayer 124

Part 3: Practices 144

Chapter 8: Clarifying the Purpose 145

Chapter 9: Practical Organization 153

Chapter 10: Pastoral Care 171

Chapter 11: Multiplication 188

Part 4: Challenges and Encouragement 210

Chapter 12: Mission 211

Chapter 13: Challenges and Conflict 223

Conclusion: Faithful Leadership in Small Groups.................236

Bibliography 240

Appendices **251**

Appendix 1 252

Appendix 2 253

Appendix 3 254

Appendix 4 255

Appendix 5 256

Appendix 6 257

About The Author 260

Preface

Jesus gave His followers a clear and timeless command: *"Go therefore and make disciples of all nations, baptizing them: teaching them to observe all that I have commanded you"* (Matthew 28:19–20, ESV). The call to discipleship is at the very heart of the Great Commission, and I believe one of the most effective ways the local church can live out this mission is through healthy, biblical small groups.

Over the years, God has given me the honor and privilege of serving in small group ministry leadership across multiple churches. In that journey, I have witnessed firsthand the power of groups to foster spiritual growth, multiply leaders, and send disciples into mission. My passion and the reason this book exists is to equip small group leaders with practical, biblical guidance for leading in a way that helps their groups thrive.

This book is born out of years of training, practice, and learning alongside small group leaders. It is designed to be a tool—a guide you can return to often—as you shepherd people toward maturity in Christ. My prayer is that it will encourage you, challenge you, and provide biblical insight into the sacred work of disciple-making.

As you begin with the introduction, you will find practical help on how to use this resource. But before you turn the page, I want to invite you to pause and pray. Ask the Lord to open your heart, renew your vision, and strengthen your hands for the work of leading others in discipleship. Remember the words of the apostle Paul: *"Him we proclaim, warning everyone and teaching everyone with all wisdom, that we may present everyone mature in Christ. For this I toil, struggling*

with all his energy that he powerfully works within me"
(Colossians 1:28–29, ESV).

May the Lord bless you as you lead, and may your group become a place where disciples are made, leaders are developed, and the mission of God continues to multiply.

Serving together in Christ,

Kent Shepherd

Introduction: Why Small Groups Matter

Small groups are the lifeblood of the local church. Throughout history, they have served as the front door of the church—often before believers ever entered a worship gathering. In small groups, discipleship takes root, accountability is embraced, and spiritual formation is cultivated. If you are reading this book, it likely means you serve in some capacity in small group ministry, as a pastor, ministry director, or teacher. This book is written with you in mind. It is not only designed to help you oversee a small group ministry but also to equip you personally to lead a healthy, growing, biblically grounded small group.

Jesus' Model

Every great movement of God begins small. Jesus Himself chose not to build His kingdom through political structures, social power, or grand institutions. Instead, He called a small band of ordinary men to Himself. *"And he went up on the mountain and called to him those whom he desired, and they came to him. And he appointed twelve (whom he also named apostles) so that they might be with him and he might send them out to preach and have authority to cast out demons"* (Mark 3:13–15, ESV).

Notice the simplicity of His method: He called them to be with Him and then sent them out. Before they preached, healed, or led others, they first lived in close fellowship with Christ and with one another. This small group became the training ground for mission. Jesus modeled life with them—

teaching them the Scriptures, praying with them, sharing meals, correcting and encouraging them. Through this investment, the Twelve were transformed from fishermen and tax collectors into world changers.

The Early Church Pattern

The apostles carried forward this model. After Pentecost, the explosive growth of the church in Jerusalem was not sustained by large gatherings alone. Scripture tells us: *"And they devoted themselves to the apostles' teaching and the fellowship, to the breaking of bread and the prayers…And day by day, attending the temple together and breaking bread in their homes, they received their food with glad and generous hearts"* (Acts 2:42, 46, ESV).

Two patterns emerge: they gathered publicly in the temple courts for worship, and they gathered privately in homes for discipleship. The large gathering was essential for proclaiming Christ, but the smaller gatherings were where believers were discipled, cared for, and equipped. In these circles, they shared life, studied the Word, confessed sins, prayed together, and met one another's needs. The church grew not only in number but in depth, because discipleship was embedded into daily life.

The pattern repeats throughout the New Testament. Paul taught "publicly and from house to house" (Acts 20:20). Aquila and Priscilla discipled Apollos in a smaller setting (Acts 18:26). Churches often met in homes—whether in Corinth (1 Corinthians 16:19), Rome (Romans 16:5), or Colossae (Colossians 4:15). The biblical witness is clear: discipleship thrives in community, and community flourishes in small gatherings.

A Modern Echo: Arthur Flake's Vision

Centuries later, this biblical foundation found fresh expression in the work of Arthur Flake (1862–1952), a layman turned leader in the Southern Baptist Convention. Flake believed that Sunday School, and by extension small groups, were not merely a program but the very heartbeat of the church's mission. His "Five Principles" (knowing the possibilities, enlarging the organization, providing space, enlisting and training workers, and going after the people) emphasized that growth in the church comes through intentional discipleship in smaller circles.

Flake insisted that the church must be organized to care for people personally, not just gathered to hear preaching. He often said, "You build people by building groups." His vision helped launch a small group movement that equipped ordinary Christians to teach, shepherd, and multiply disciples.[1] Like Barnabas in the New Testament, Flake saw the power of encouragement, organization, and multiplication as essential to a thriving church.

Flake's influence remains a reminder: small groups are not a secondary ministry of the church. They are the church—meeting faithfully in homes, classrooms, and circles where lives are transformed.

---

[1] See J. N. (Arthur) Flake, *Building a Standard Sunday School* (Nashville: Sunday School Board of the Southern Baptist Convention, 1922).

Why Small Groups Matter Today

The church today faces the same challenge as the early church: How do we move people from being consumers in a crowd to disciples in community? Worship services are vital, but they cannot carry the full weight of discipleship. In a crowd, people can remain anonymous. In a small group, anonymity disappears, and accountability begins.

Small groups serve as vital environments where the core practices of Christian life are lived out in community. They are the primary place where **discipleship** happens as believers are equipped to follow Christ through studying His Word, applying biblical truth, and encouraging one another in obedience. Within these groups, **accountability** also takes shape as truth is spoken in love and members challenge and support one another toward growth in Christlikeness. Beyond knowledge, small groups provide a space for **spiritual formation**, helping people not only understand what the Bible says but also put it into practice in daily life. They become training grounds for living out faith in tangible ways. Finally, small groups embrace the **mission** of God together by praying for the lost, serving in their communities, and actively participating in the Great Commission. In this way, they are not only about gathering but also about sending: equipping disciples to live faithfully in their neighborhoods, workplaces, and beyond.

Healthy small groups are not optional; they are essential. Without them, discipleship becomes shallow, relationships stay surface-level, and mission drifts to the margins. With them, the church becomes a multiplying movement of people who know God deeply, grow together in authentic community, and live sent into the world.

Outline of the Book

This book is written to equip you as a small group leader and to encourage you in the vital ministry you carry. It is structured into four parts:

- **Part 1: Foundations:** The biblical and theological basis for small groups.
- **Part 2: Principles:** The essential skills of preparation, presentation, participation, and prayer.
- **Part 3: Practices:** The practical rhythms that keep groups healthy and multiplying: clarifying purpose, organizing effectively, shepherding faithfully, and raising leaders.
- **Part 4: Challenges and Encouragement:** Facing the inevitable challenges of small group life, staying outward-focused in mission, and persevering with hope.

Each chapter grounds you in Scripture, draws from the wisdom of leaders who have gone before, and provides practical tools you can apply immediately to your small group. Along the way, you will also encounter reflection questions to deepen your personal growth and action steps that help translate insight into practice. Whether you are a new leader learning the basics or a seasoned shepherd seeking fresh encouragement, each chapter is designed to equip you with both confidence and direction for leading well.

A Word to Leaders

If you are leading a group or overseeing many groups, you are standing in a line of disciple-makers that stretches back to Jesus Himself, through the early church, through faithful men such as Arthur Flake, and now through your own ministry.

Your calling is not small. As Paul wrote, *"Let us not grow weary of doing good, for in due season we will reap, if we do not give up"* (Galatians 6:9, ESV). The Lord has entrusted people to your care. This book is here to strengthen your hands, deepen your heart, and encourage your soul as you lead God's people.

Part 1: Foundations

Chapter 1: The Biblical Foundation of Small Groups

"And they devoted themselves to the apostles' teaching and the fellowship, to the breaking of bread and the prayers…And the Lord added to their number day by day those who were being saved."—Acts 2:42, 47 (ESV)

A Return to the Early Church Model

From the very beginning of God's story, community was never optional. In the Old Testament, Israel was called to be a people who lived together under God's covenant. Moses urged parents to teach their children diligently *"when you sit in your house, and when you walk by the way, and when you lie down, and when you rise"* (Deuteronomy 6:7, ESV). Even Moses himself organized Israel into smaller groups of tens, fifties, and hundreds so that people could be shepherded more effectively (Exodus 18:21–25).

When Luke describes the early believers in Jerusalem, he is not giving us a quaint picture of fellowship dinners but a Holy Spirit-filled people who gathered in homes, broke bread, prayed together, and shared their lives. Their common devotion to Christ overflowed into devotion to one another (Acts 2:42–47).

This is not just a historical snapshot; it is a biblical blueprint. Small groups were the heartbeat of the early church's growth and multiplication. They were not programs invented to keep believers busy; they were the natural outworking of the gospel in community.

In my own ministry, I have had the privilege of overseeing small group ministry in three different churches. Over the years, I have witnessed the unique blessing of what God does in these settings. While corporate worship inspires and unites, there is a depth of accountability, transformation, and mission that happens more naturally in a small group. Some of the greatest moments of spiritual growth I have seen occurred not in a sanctuary, but in a living room.[2]

Jesus' Example of Small-Group Discipleship

Even before the church was born at Pentecost, Jesus Himself modeled the power of a small group. Though He ministered to multitudes, He chose twelve disciples to live closely with Him. Mark records: *"And he appointed twelve (whom he also named apostles) so that they might be with him and he might send them out to preach and have authority to cast out demons"* (Mark 3:14–15, ESV).

---

[2] See Jeffrey Arnold, *The Big Book on Small Groups* (rev. ed.; Downers Grove, IL: InterVarsity Press, 2001); Andy Stanley and Bill Willits, *Creating Community: Five Keys to Building a Small Group Culture* (Colorado Springs: Multnomah, 2004); Larry Osborne, *Sticky Church* (Grand Rapids: Zondervan, 2008); Ben Sobels and Colin Marshall, *The Trellis and the Vine: The Ministry Mind-Shift That Changes Everything* (Kingsford, Australia: Matthias Media, 2009); Bill Donahue, *Building a Church of Small Groups: A Place Where Nobody Stands Alone* (Grand Rapids: Zondervan, 2001); Ed Stetzer and Eric Geiger, *Transformational Groups: Creating a New Scorecard for Groups* (Nashville: B&H, 2014).

Here we see life-on-life discipleship at work. Jesus taught them privately, corrected them lovingly, and sent them out with purpose. Transformation rarely happens in a crowd; it happens in smaller circles where believers are truly known, shepherded, and equipped. Rows may inspire, but circles transform.[3]

Small Groups in the Old Testament

While the New Testament gives us the clearest picture of small groups in action, the foundation is already laid in the Old Testament. God has always worked through His people in community, not in isolation.

- **Discipleship in the Dwelling:** The Shema in Deuteronomy 6 shows that spiritual formation begins in the home: *"You shall teach them diligently to your children, and shall talk of them when you sit in your house, and when you walk by the way, and when you lie down, and when you rise"* (Deuteronomy 6:7, ESV). This was not a lecture in the temple courts but daily discipleship in the rhythms of family life.

- **Delegation in the Desert:** When Moses grew weary from judging the people alone, Jethro counseled him to appoint leaders over *"thousands, hundreds, fifties, and tens"* (Exodus 18:21). God's people were shepherded best when they were divided into smaller, more relational groups under shared leadership.

---

[3] See Arnold, *Big Book on Small Groups*; Stanley and Willits, *Creating Community*; Osborne, *Sticky Church*; Marshall and Sobels, *Trellis and the Vine*; Donahue, *Building a Church of Small Groups*; Stetzer and Geiger, *Transformational Groups*.

- **Dependence in Daily Life:** Ecclesiastes reminds us of the power of companionship: *"Two are better than one… For if they fall, one will lift up his fellow…a threefold cord is not quickly broken"* (Ecclesiastes 4:9–12). The principle of mutual support and accountability has always been God's design.

The Old Testament reveals that small, relational gatherings were central to God's covenant community. These patterns anticipate what would become the heartbeat of the New Testament church. From the earliest days, Israel gathered in homes, families, and villages to hear God's Word and to remember His covenant faithfulness. These smaller circles allowed God's people not only to worship together but also to encourage one another, pass on the faith to the next generation, and walk in accountability. Later, the synagogue model gave further shape to these rhythms of fellowship, prayer, and Scripture-centered teaching. Thus, when the early church began meeting in homes (Acts 2:46), they were not inventing something new but stepping into the rich heritage of God's design for community life.[4]

Small Groups in the Epistles

The letters of Paul and other apostles assume the presence of small gatherings. While the gospel was proclaimed publicly, discipleship was lived out in homes.

- **Churches Met in Houses:** Paul greets *"the church in their house"* (Romans 16:5; 1 Corinthians 16:19;

---

[4] See Arnold, *Big Book on Small Groups*; Stanley and Willits, *Creating Community*; Osborne, *Sticky Church*; Marshall and Sobels, *Trellis and the Vine*; Donahue, *Building a Church of Small Groups*; Stetzer and Geiger, *Transformational Groups*.

Colossians 4:15; Philemon 2). Before cathedrals and auditoriums, the church grew in living rooms. These house churches provided the relational environment where the gospel could be taught, applied, and shared.

- **Close-Knit Fellowship:** The epistles are filled with instructions that make sense only in smaller communities. Paul exhorts believers to *"admonish one another"* (Colossians 3:16), *"comfort one another"* (1 Thessalonians 4:18), and *"confess your sins to one another"* (James 5:16). These are intimate commands that require proximity and trust.

- **Leadership Development:** Paul's pattern with Timothy and Titus shows how leaders were identified, trained, and released in the context of local gatherings. The home served as both sanctuary and training ground.

The New Testament confirms that biblical Christianity was never designed to be anonymous. The faith was lived out in households, where people knew one another deeply and carried out Christ's commands together.[5] We are reminded throughout Acts and the Epistles that believers are to grow in their walk with Christ together. This growth comes through accountability, encouragement, study, and fellowship.

Why Small Groups Matter Today

In a culture that prizes independence yet suffers from deep loneliness, the church must reclaim the richness of biblical

----

[5] See Arnold, *Big Book on Small Groups*; Stanley and Willits, *Creating Community*; Osborne, *Sticky Church*; Marshall and Sobels, *Trellis and the Vine*; Donahue, *Building a Church of Small Groups*; Stetzer and Geiger, *Transformational Groups*.

community. Jesus calls His followers to be *"the salt of the earth"* and *"the light of the world"* (Matthew 5:13–16), shining His truth and love in a society that often hides behind social media, shallow connections, and false identities. Small groups matter because they:

Grow Believers: James exhorts us to be *"doers of the word, and not hearers only"* (James 1:22, ESV). Small groups create an environment where Scripture can be wrestled with, applied, and lived out in accountable relationships. Growth happens when truth is not only heard but obeyed together.

Guard Fellowship: Hebrews reminds us to *"consider how to stir up one another to love and good works, not neglecting to meet together"* (Hebrews 10:24–25, ESV). Small groups guard against isolation by fostering encouragement, prayer, and genuine care. They provide a place where believers carry one another's burdens (Galatians 6:2).

Give Witness: The book of Acts shows that community life was itself a powerful testimony, *"the Lord added to their number day by day those who were being saved"* (Acts 2:47, ESV). Today, research confirms what Scripture already teaches; many unchurched people would attend a group if invited. Small groups are frontline mission posts, where neighbors, coworkers, and friends can experience the love of Christ.

Generate Leaders: Small groups are catalysts for leadership. As David Francis notes, "The presence of an apprentice leader is the clearest sign of a group's commitment to reaching others."[6] Groups are incubators for shepherds, teachers, and disciple-makers.

The "One Anothers" of the New Testament

One of the clearest biblical pictures of why small groups matter comes from the *"one another"* commands of the New Testament. Over fifty times, the writers of Scripture instruct believers how to treat one another. These commands cannot be obeyed in isolation or in a large crowd alone; they require the intimacy of smaller gatherings where relationships are genuine and discipleship is personal. To make them memorable, we have grouped these *"one anothers"* into three categories, Care, Comfort, and Confess.

The "One Anothers" of the New Testament Chart

Handle	Practical Commands	Scripture References
Care for One Another	Love, serve, forgive, show hospitality	John 13:34; Gal. 5:13; Eph. 4:32; 1 Pet. 4:9
Comfort One Another	Encourage, build up, bear burdens	1 Thess. 5:11; Gal. 6:2
Confess to One Another	Teach, admonish, confess sins, and pray	Col. 3:16; Jas. 5:16

The *"one anothers"* remind us that Christianity is not just about believing—it is about belonging. To love, serve, encourage, and pray for one another requires more than a weekly worship service; it requires life together in community. Rows can hear sermons, but circles are where the *"one anothers"* are lived out. Small groups provide the environment

---

[6] David Francis, *The Discover Triad: Three Facets of a Dynamic Adult Class* (Nashville: LifeWay, 2012), 19.

where these commands become more than words on a page—they become the lived reality of God's people.[7]

Principles, Not Just Methods

It is easy to think of small groups in terms of methods—curriculum, format, or schedule. But methods change with time and culture. Homes may give way to coffee shops, and printed studies to digital ones. Principles, however, are timeless. Harrington Emerson observed: "Methods are many. Principles are few. Methods always change. Principles never do."[8]

The Principles That Shape Biblical Small Groups[9]

1. Scripture as the Foundation: God's Word is the bedrock of any biblical small group. Without it, groups drift into opinion-sharing rather than transformation. Paul reminded Timothy that *"All Scripture is breathed out by God and profitable for teaching, for reproof, for correction, and for training in righteousness"* (2 Timothy 3:16, ESV). Jesus

---

[7] See Jeffrey Arnold, *The Big Book on Small Groups*, rev. ed. (Downers Grove, IL: InterVarsity Press, 2001); Andy Stanley and Bill Willits, *Creating Community: Five Keys to Building a Small Group Culture* (Colorado Springs: Multnomah, 2004); Larry Osborne, *Sticky Church* (Grand Rapids: Zondervan, 2008); Bill Donahue, *Building a Church of Small Groups: A Place Where Nobody Stands Alone* (Grand Rapids: Zondervan, 2001); Ed Stetzer and Eric Geiger, *Transformational Groups: Creating a New Scorecard for Groups* (Nashville: B&H, 2014).

[8] Harrington Emerson, *Twelve Principles of Efficiency* (New York: The Engineering Magazine, 1912), 13.

[9] See Arnold, *Big Book on Small Groups*; Stanley and Willits, *Creating Community*; Osborne, *Sticky Church*; Donahue, *Building a Church of Small Groups*; Stetzer and Geiger, *Transformational Groups*.

Himself declared, *"Sanctify them in the truth; your word is truth"* (John 17:17).

Leader Tip: Center your group on the text. Ask three simple questions; What does it say? What does it mean? How should we live it?

2. Prayer as the Power: If Scripture provides the foundation, prayer provides the power. Small groups thrive when prayer is not a formality but the lifeblood of their gatherings. *"They devoted themselves…to the prayers"* (Acts 2:42). Jesus promised, *"For where two or three are gathered in my name, there am I among them"* (Matthew 18:20).

Leader Tip: Build prayer into the rhythm of your group. Share needs openly. Pray specifically. Rotate who leads prayer so dependence is shared.

3. Community as the Environment: The Christian life was never meant to be lived in isolation. *"Two are better than one…for if they fall, one will lift up his fellow"* (Ecclesiastes 4:9–10). Hebrews exhorts us to encourage one another daily (Hebrews 10:24–25). Just as the early believers shared meals, possessions, and burdens (Acts 2:44–47), small groups today provide a context where genuine fellowship happens.

Leader Tip: Create space for people to be real. Ask good questions. Eat together. Celebrate together and carry one another's burdens.

4. Mission as the Goal: A small group that only looks inward loses sight of God's purpose. Jesus' final command was, *"Go therefore and make disciples of all nations"*

(Matthew 28:19). Acts 1:8 reminds us that the Spirit empowers believers to be witnesses "to the end of the earth."

Leader Tip: Keep chairs open. Regularly ask: Whom can we invite? Where can we serve? How can we multiply?

The Dangers of Neglecting Biblical Community

When the church neglects biblical small groups, the consequences are serious:[10]

- **Without Scripture**, groups drift into opinion and error. God warned of a *"famine of hearing the words of the Lord"* (Amos 8:11). Without the Word, people are malnourished.

- **Without Prayer**, groups operate in human strength. *"Not by might, nor by power, but by my Spirit, says the Lord of hosts"* (Zechariah 4:6). Prayerless groups are powerless groups.

- **Without Community**, believers are isolated and vulnerable. *"Woe to him who is alone when he falls and has not another to lift him up"* (Ecclesiastes 4:10). Isolation breeds discouragement and temptation.

- **Without Mission**, groups stagnate. Jesus rebuked the church at Sardis for having *"the reputation of being alive, but you are dead"* (Revelation 3:1). Groups that exist only for themselves lose gospel vitality. Neglecting

---

[10] See Sobels and Marshall, *Trellis and the Vine*; Donahue, *Building a Church of Small Groups*; Stetzer and Geiger, *Transformational Groups*.

community is not neutral—it weakens witness, discipleship, and the health of the whole body.

Snapshots of the Early Church

The book of Acts gives us vivid glimpses of the earliest groups. These first gatherings of believers were not casual, they were central to the life of the church. These early snapshots remind us that biblical small groups are not a modern strategy but God's original design for His people to grow, serve, and carry out His mission.

- **They learned together:** Believers were devoted to the apostles' teaching (Acts 2:42).
- **They lived together:** The early church shared meals and possessions (Acts 2:44–46).
- **They prayed together:** They interceded as one body (Acts 4:24).
- **They served together:** Early church meet needs as they arose (Acts 6:1–6).
- **They witnessed together:** The Lord added daily (Acts 2:47).

This rhythm of shared life was not merely cultural but the God-ordained soil where disciples multiplied and churches were planted. Their unity and generosity created an environment where *"the Lord added to their number day by day those who were being saved"* (Acts 2:47, ESV). Paul affirmed this principle when he described how the Thessalonians became *"an example to all the believers in Macedonia and in Achaia"* (1 Thessalonians 1:7). Biblical community is never stagnant; it is fertile ground where disciples grow and churches take root.[11]

Practical Rhythms of a Healthy Group

What does a healthy small group look like in practice? Acts 2:42–47 provides the template.

- **Gather around the Word:** Center meetings on Scripture (Acts 2:42). Scripture is opened and discussed, not just taught. Everyone participates.

- **Go to God in Prayer:** Pray dependently and consistently (Acts 4:24). Needs are shared honestly, and prayer is given priority.

- **Grow through Fellowship:** Share life authentically (Acts 2:44–46). Share meals, celebrations, and burdens as part of the rhythm. The group becomes family.

- **Give in Service:** Groups look outward by meeting needs in the church and community (Acts 6:1–6).

- **Go Multiply:** Healthy groups raise up leaders and send them out to begin new groups, just as the gospel spread in Acts (Acts 9:31).

These rhythms ensure that small groups are not just meetings on a calendar but environments of transformation.[12]

---

[11] John B. Polhill, *Acts, vol. 26 in The New American Commentary* (Nashville: Broadman, 1992), 242–47.

[12] Polhill, *Acts*, 242–47.

Stories from Church History

Throughout history, God has used small groups to spark renewal and advance the mission of the Church. The following are examples of small groups within the church that ignited revival in their communities and even influenced the world. This serves as a powerful reminder that God delights in using ordinary people to accomplish extraordinary things. In the same way, He can use a small group like the one you lead to bring lasting change to the world.

- **The Early Church:** House gatherings fueled the spread of the gospel across the Roman Empire despite persecution.[13]

- **The Moravians:** In the 1700s, a small community in Herrnhut, Germany, committed to round-the-clock prayer in groups. That prayer meeting lasted over 100 years and launched one of the greatest missionary movements in history.[14]

- **The Wesleyan Revival:** John Wesley's "class meetings" in England were small groups for accountability and discipleship. These small groups became the engine of Methodist renewal and social transformation.[15]

---

[13] Polhill, *Acts*, 242–47.

[14] "The One Hundred Year Prayer Meeting," *Christian History Institute*, accessed August 21, 2025, https://christianhistoryinstitute.org/magazine/article/one-hundred-year-prayer-meeting.

[15] "John Wesley and Small Groups," *Conciliar Post*, accessed August 21, 2025, https://conciliarpost.com/christian-traditions/methodist/john-wesley-and-small-groups/.

From Jerusalem to Herrnhut to England, history shows the same truth. When God's people gather in small, devoted communities, revival often follows. These movements remind us that God still delights to work through ordinary believers who are faithful together in prayer, Scripture, and mission.

A Call to Leaders

If you are a small group leader, you are stepping into one of the most strategic roles in the life of the church. You are not simply facilitating a discussion; you are cultivating an environment where the Spirit of God transforms lives. When you open your home or lead a group, you stand in the same stream of history as Jesus with His twelve, the believers gathered in homes in Acts, and the house churches that spread across the Roman Empire. Every small group is a seedbed of gospel transformation. A place where the lost meet Christ, the lonely find belonging, and believers grow to maturity.

The question, then, is not whether small groups matter. Scripture has already settled that subject. The real question is: Will we steward them faithfully, biblically, and intentionally for the glory of God and the growth of His people?

Obstacles to Biblical Small Groups

Even with biblical clarity, groups will face challenges. Leaders must be ready to anticipate these difficulties and shepherd people through them. A good leader does not ignore obstacles within the group but addresses them with wisdom and care.

- **Busyness:** People feel they don't have time. Yet Hebrews 10:25 reminds us not to neglect meeting together. Leaders must model prioritizing spiritual community over convenience.

- **Barriers of Fear:** Some hesitate to share openly. Leaders can set the tone by modeling honesty and grace (2 Corinthians 12:9).

- **Bound by Consumerism:** Many approach groups asking, "What will I get?" rather than, "How can I give?" Paul calls believers to *"look not only to his own interests, but also to the interests of others"* (Philippians 2:4).

- **Breakdown in Leadership:** Without trained leaders, groups falter. Paul's charge to Timothy—*"what you have heard...entrust to faithful men"* (2 Timothy 2:2)—shows the importance of apprenticing new leaders.

Obstacles are real, but they are not insurmountable. With biblical conviction, patient leadership, and reliance on the Spirit, groups can overcome these challenges and thrive.[16]

Reflection Questions

1. What stands out to you about the model of community in Acts 2:42–47? How does it challenge your view of the church today?

2. Why do you think Jesus invested in twelve disciples rather than focusing only on the crowds? What does this teach us about discipleship?

---

[16] See Arnold, *Big Book on Small Groups*; Stanley and Willits, *Creating Community*; Osborne, *Sticky Church*; Donahue, *Building a Church of Small Groups*; Stetzer and Geiger, *Transformational Groups*.

3. Which of the four principles (Scripture, prayer, community, mission) does your group most need to strengthen? Why?

4. If someone visited your group for the first time, what would they learn about Christ by the way you live together?

5. What steps could you take as a leader (or participant) to make your group more like the early church — devoted, prayerful, generous, and mission-focused?

Chapter 2: The Character of the Small Group Leader

"Shepherd the flock of God that is among you, exercising oversight, not under compulsion, but willingly, as God would have you; not for shameful gain, but eagerly; not domineering over those in your charge, but being examples to the flock."— 1 Peter 5:2–3 (ESV)

Leadership Begins with Character

The most important resource of any small group is not the curriculum, the meeting location, or the size of the group; it is the leader. A group will rarely rise above the spiritual health of its shepherd. For that reason, the call to small group leadership is not simply about facilitation or organization; it is first a call to godly character.

Scripture emphasizes this in every description of church leadership. Paul's letters to Timothy and Titus highlight qualities such as integrity, hospitality, self-control, and faithfulness (1 Timothy 3:1–7; Titus 1:6–9). Small group leaders may not all carry the title of elder, but they carry the same responsibility of modeling a life worthy of imitation.[17]

---

[17] See J. Oswald Sanders, *Spiritual Leadership: Principles of Excellence for Every Believer* (rev. ed.; Chicago: Moody, 2007); John MacArthur, *The Book on Leadership* (Nashville: Thomas Nelson, 2004); Gene A. Getz, *Elders and Leaders: God's Plan for Leading the Church* (Chicago: Moody, 2003); A. W. Tozer, *The Knowledge of the Holy* (New York: Harper & Row, 1961); John Piper, *Brothers, We Are Not Professionals: A Plea to Pastors for Radical Ministry* (Nashville: B&H, 2002); and R. Kent Hughes, *Liberating Ministry from the Success Syndrome* (Wheaton: Crossway, 1987).

J.R. Miller once wrote, "The real power in teaching is not in methods, important as these are; nor in equipment, valuable as this is — but in the teacher's own spiritual life. 'Not by might, nor by power, but by my Spirit,' is the divine revealing of the secret of power in all Christian work."[18]

Your leadership rises and falls not on your cleverness but on your Christlikeness. A small group will rarely grow deeper than its leader's own walk with God.

Essential Qualities of a Leader

The foundation of small group leadership is not primarily skill but character. Skills can be taught, but character must be cultivated. The following five qualities—spiritual maturity, integrity, humility, teachability, and a shepherding heart—reflect the biblical vision of leadership.[19]

1. Spiritual Maturity: A leader must first be a growing disciple before guiding others. Leaders cannot give what they do not possess. Jesus reminded His disciples, *"I am the vine; you are the branches. Whoever abides in me and I in him, he it is that bears much fruit, for apart from me you can do nothing"* (John 15:5). Fruitful leadership flows from abiding in Christ.

Paul warned Timothy to *"keep a close watch on yourself and on the teaching"* (1 Timothy 4:16). Before leaders watch over others, they must watch over their own spiritual health. A lukewarm leader, halfhearted in prayer, Scripture, or obedience

18 J. R. Miller, *Personal Friendships of Jesus* (New York: Thomas Y. Crowell, 1897), 112

19 See Sanders, *Spiritual Leadership*; MacArthur, *Book on Leadership*; Getz, *Elders and Leaders*; Tozer, *Knowledge of the Holy*; Piper, *Brothers, We Are Not Professionals*; Hughes, *Liberating Ministry*.

will inevitably reproduce lukewarmness in others (Revelation 3:16).

Richard Baxter, the Puritan pastor, urged ministers, "Take heed to yourselves, lest you should be void of that saving grace of God which you offer to others…and lest you should famish yourselves while you prepare them food."[20] Leaders must model a vibrant walk with God, demonstrating daily dependence on Scripture, prayer, and obedience.

2. Integrity: Integrity means wholeness, a life consistent in both public and private. Scripture repeatedly affirms this principle, *"The righteous who walks in his integrity—blessed are his children after him!"* (Proverbs 20:7).

Paul required overseers to be "above reproach" (1 Timothy 3:2). This does not mean perfection, but a life without hypocrisy. Jesus condemned the Pharisees not for lack of knowledge but for lack of integrity: *"They preach, but do not practice"* (Matthew 23:3). Nothing erodes trust in leadership faster than hypocrisy. Howard Hendricks observed, "You cannot impart what you do not possess. You cannot communicate out of a vacuum. What you are is more important than what you say."[21] A leader of integrity models consistency between word and deed, doctrine and practice, public ministry and private devotion.

3. Humility: Biblical leadership is never about self-promotion but about serving others. Jesus taught, *"Whoever would be great among you must be your servant"* (Matthew

---

[20] Richard Baxter, *The Reformed Pastor* (1656; repr., Edinburgh: Banner of Truth, 1974), 62.

[21] Howard Hendricks, *Teaching to Change Lives* (Portland: Multnomah, 1987), 15.

20:26). True greatness in God's kingdom is measured not by authority but by humility.

Paul exhorted believers, *"Do nothing from selfish ambition or conceit, but in humility count others more significant than yourselves"* (Philippians 2:3). He then pointed to Christ Himself, who *"emptied himself, by taking the form of a servant"* (Philippians 2:7).

Andrew Murray captured this well, "Pride must die in you, or nothing of heaven can live in you."[22] A humble leader is quick to listen, slow to speak, and eager to serve. Humility opens the door for God's grace. Scripture reminds us: *"God opposes the proud but gives grace to the humble"* (James 4:6).

4. Teachability: Effective leaders remain lifelong learners. Proverbs teaches, *"The way of a fool is right in his own eyes, but a wise man listens to advice"* (Proverbs 12:15). Leaders who are unwilling to receive correction or feedback will eventually stagnate and lead their people into the same complacency.

Paul himself modeled teachability. Though an apostle, he admitted, *"Not that I have already obtained this or am already perfect, but I press on to make it my own"* (Philippians 3:12). Leaders who admit their need for growth inspire their groups to pursue Christ with humility.

Ken Blanchard and Phil Hodges stress this principle: "The servant leader constantly seeks feedback because the goal is

---

[22] Andrew Murray, *Humility: The Beauty of Holiness* (New Kensington, PA: Whitaker House, 1982), 12.

not to protect image but to grow in effectiveness for Christ."[23] A teachable leader creates a culture where growth, not pride, is the norm. Leaders who are humble are teachable.

5. Shepherding Heart: Leadership in the church is not about managing programs but shepherding people. Jesus declared Himself the Good Shepherd who *"lays down his life for the sheep"* (John 10:11). Small group leaders reflect His heart when they care for the people entrusted to them.

Peter's exhortation captures this well: *"Shepherd the flock of God that is among you, exercising oversight...not domineering over those in your charge, but being examples to the flock"* (1 Peter 5:2–3). Paul mirrored this when he described his ministry to the Thessalonians, *"We were gentle among you, like a nursing mother taking care of her own children"* (1 Thessalonians 2:7).

A shepherding heart is patient in trials, tender in encouragement, and persistent in prayer. Leaders walk with people not only in spiritual victories but also in struggles, embodying Christ's compassion and care.

The essential qualities of a small group leader—spiritual maturity, integrity, humility, teachability, and a shepherding heart—are not optional traits; they are biblical necessities. Methods may vary, but these character traits remain timeless. A leader who embodies these qualities reflects the heart of Christ,

---

[23] Ken Blanchard and Phil Hodges, *The Servant Leader* (Nashville: Thomas Nelson, 2003), 56.

builds trust with their group, and creates an environment where discipleship flourishes.[24]

A Leader's Heart Check

- Am I spending daily time with the Lord?
- Do I model obedience to Scripture in front of others?
- Is my leadership marked more by serving than by controlling?
- Do I seek accountability for my weaknesses?
- Do I pray regularly for the members of my group by name?

Grounded in the Word

Paul reminded Timothy that *"all Scripture is breathed out by God and profitable for teaching, for reproof, for correction, and for training in righteousness"* (2 Timothy 3:16). Leaders must first allow the Word to shape their own hearts before they attempt to shape others.

A biblically grounded leader understands that the authority of their leadership does not rest on personality, experience, or skill, but on the Word of God. Such a leader **approaches Scripture with careful study**, first asking, "What did this mean then and there?" before jumping to 'What does this mean

---

[24] See Sanders, *Spiritual Leadership*; MacArthur, *Book on Leadership*; Getz, *Elders and Leaders*; Tozer, *Knowledge of the Holy*; Piper, *Brothers, We Are Not Professionals*; Hughes, *Liberating Ministry*.

here and now?'"[25] This discipline ensures that the message is faithful to its original context and intent, guarding against misinterpretation or the temptation to twist Scripture to fit personal preferences. By grounding their teaching in the historical and literary setting of the text, leaders provide a solid foundation for application in the lives of their group members today.

Yet study alone is not enough. A biblically grounded leader also **prays for a teachable spirit**, recognizing that true understanding comes only through the illumination of the Holy Spirit. Humility is key here. Leaders do not come to the Bible as masters but as students, dependent on God to open their eyes to His truth. This posture of prayerful dependence not only shapes their personal study but also models for their group what it means to submit to God's authority.

Finally, a biblically grounded leader must be willing to **apply the text personally**. They allow the Holy Spirit to convict, correct, and encourage them before they ever ask the group to follow suit. Leadership marked by authenticity and transformation is far more compelling than leadership that merely instructs others. When leaders live under the authority of Scripture, their lives become living testimonies of God's power to change hearts. In this way, they not only teach the Bible but embody its truth, showing their group that discipleship is about obedience, not just information.

As Gordon Fee and Douglas Stuart warn: "To make a text mean something God did not intend is to abuse the text, not use

---

[25] See Gordon D. Fee and Douglas Stuart, *How to Read the Bible for All Its Worth,* 3rd ed. (Grand Rapids: Zondervan, 2003).

it."[26] Leaders carry the sacred responsibility of rightly handling the Word of truth (2 Timothy 2:15).[27]

Rooted in Prayer

If Scripture forms the foundation, prayer fuels the work. E. M. Bounds described prayer as: "Communion and fellowship with God, the enjoyment of God, and access to God."[28]

Leaders who neglect prayer may still lead a meeting, but they cannot lead a movement of God. Jesus warned against empty, self-seeking prayers (Matthew 6:5–7). Instead, prayer should be God-centered, *"Your kingdom come, your will be done"* (Matthew 6:10). J. C. Ryle famously pressed the question: "Do you pray?"[29] For him, prayer was not saying words but living in dependence on God. A prayerful leader does the following:

- Prays for their own spiritual health.
- Prays for group members by name.
- Prays during preparation and while leading.
- Teaches the group how to pray—individually, corporately, and even through prayer-walking.

---

[26] Gordon D. Fee and Douglas Stuart, *How to Read the Bible for All Its Worth,* 3rd ed. (Grand Rapids: Zondervan, 2003), 29.

[27] See Sanders, *Spiritual Leadership*; MacArthur, *Book on Leadership*; Getz, *Elders and Leaders*; Tozer, *Knowledge of the Holy*; Piper, *Brothers, We Are Not Professionals*; Hughes, *Liberating Ministry.*

[28] E. M. Bounds, *The Complete Works of E. M. Bounds on Prayer* (Grand Rapids: Baker, 1990), 377.

[29] J. C. Ryle, *A Call to Prayer* (London: William Hunt, 1878), 3.

Prayer is not an accessory to leadership; it is the atmosphere in which leadership breathes. It shapes our perspective, humbles our hearts, and aligns our will with God's purposes (Matthew 6:5–15). Prayer is our direct line of communication with the Lord, and as leaders, we must depend on Him through prayer.

Healthy in Spirit, Mind, and Body

Small group leaders carry weight—spiritual, emotional, and mental. Many leaders burn out not because they don't love God, but because they fail to guard their health. Peter Scazzero reminds us, "We cannot give what we do not possess."[30]

Healthy small group leaders understand that resilience is not optional; it is crucial for long-term ministry. Resilience must be cultivated in several areas of life. **Spiritual resilience** is the foundation; rooted in Christ's peace, which guards hearts and minds beyond human understanding (Philippians 4:6–7). Leaders who anchor themselves in prayer and Scripture find a steady source of strength, even when ministry feels overwhelming. **Mental resilience** flows from this foundation and involves an honest self-awareness of personal limits, echoing the psalmist's prayer, *"Search me, O God, and know my heart"* (Psalm 139:23). By recognizing their capacity, leaders can better discern when to press forward and when to pause for renewal. **Physical resilience** is also critical, as Scripture reminds us that the body is a temple of the Holy Spirit (1 Corinthians 6:19). Honoring God with our bodies through rest, nutrition, and exercise ensures we have the stamina to serve effectively. Finally, **relational resilience** means refusing to carry the weight of ministry alone. As Paul

---

[30] Peter Scazzero, *Emotionally Healthy Spirituality* (Nashville: Thomas Nelson, 2006), 37.

teaches, believers are called to "bear one another's burdens" (Galatians 6:2). Leaders who walk with trusted friends and mentors can share both joys and challenges, reminding their groups that community is a gift of God's grace.

This holistic approach to resilience is reflected in practices like rest, setting healthy boundaries, and embracing Sabbath. Leaders who honor these rhythms demonstrate to their groups that their worth is not found in performance but in their identity in Christ (Matthew 11:28–29).[31] For many, including myself, this area can be a personal struggle. I often wrestle with the tendency to become a workaholic, pushing past my limits until my strength is depleted. Neglecting Sabbath rest leads to burnout, not fruitfulness. For this reason, I must be intentional about creating space to rest, trusting that God works even when I do not. By establishing clear boundaries, I protect my family, preserve my health, and serve from a place of overflow rather than emptiness. In doing so, I not only safeguard my own soul but also model a healthier way of leadership for those I disciple. Resilient leaders remind others that true strength comes not from constant striving, but from abiding in Christ.

Marked by Humility and Servanthood

True biblical leadership is not about control or prestige but about serving. Paul exhorted, *"Do nothing from selfish ambition or conceit, but in humility count others more significant than yourselves"* (Philippians 2:3–4). John Maxwell

---

[31] See Sanders, *Spiritual Leadership*; MacArthur, *Book on Leadership*; Getz, *Elders and Leaders*; Tozer, *Knowledge of the Holy*; Piper, *Brothers, We Are Not Professionals*; Hughes, *Liberating Ministry*.

captures this principle, "Leadership begins with authenticity and influence built through trust."[32]

A Christlike small group leader embodies the heart of servant leadership by following the example of Jesus, who came not to be served but to serve. Such a leader approaches the group with a **shepherd's heart**, guiding and caring for the flock not out of obligation but with a willing spirit (1 Peter 5:2–3). This means leadership is not about power, position, or control, but about humbly walking alongside others, nurturing their spiritual growth, and creating a safe space where members can flourish. A servant leader recognizes that the group belongs to Christ, and their role is to faithfully steward the lives entrusted to them.

Servant leadership also requires **transparency and vulnerability**. A Christlike leader models confession and accountability, living out the truth that *"iron sharpens iron"* (Proverbs 27:17). By admitting struggles and inviting accountability, leaders demonstrate that no one is above correction or beyond the need for grace. This example encourages group members to step into authenticity with one another, creating a culture where sin is confronted in love and spiritual growth is pursued together. In this way, the leader's life becomes a testimony of dependence on God and partnership with the body of Christ (James 5:16).

Finally, servant leadership in small groups keeps **multiplication at the forefront**. Leaders are not content merely to gather the same circle week after week; they take seriously the call to make disciples who make disciples (2 Timothy 2:2; Matthew 28:19–20). A Christlike leader equips

---

[32] John C. Maxwell, *The Right to Lead: A Study in Character and Courage* (Nashville: Thomas Nelson, 2001), 45.

and releases others to lead, ensuring the mission continues beyond their own influence. In doing so, they reflect the strategy of Jesus, who poured into His disciples with the expectation that they would carry the gospel to the nations. Servant leadership in small groups, then, is not about building followers for oneself but about raising up faithful disciples who will advance the kingdom of God.

Servant leadership is not weakness; it is the way of Jesus. On the night before His crucifixion, He washed His disciples' feet and commanded them to follow His example of humble service (John 13:14–15). True servant leadership means putting the needs of others before personal preferences or ambitions (Philippians 2:3–4). It does not mean the absence of leadership or authority; rather, it reflects a Christlike posture where leaders care more about the people they serve than the position they hold (Mark 10:42–45).[33]

The Leader as an Example

Paul boldly told the Corinthians, "*Be imitators of me, as I am of Christ*" (1 Corinthians 11:1). Leaders should be able to say the same. This does not mean perfection but authenticity. Members learn as much from how a leader lives as from what the person teaches.

Ken Blanchard and Phil Hodges describe servant leadership through four commitments: **Head** (vision rooted in God's mission), **Heart** (compassionate love), **Hands** (practical service), and Habits (disciplines that keep leaders centered on

---

[33] See Sanders, *Spiritual Leadership*; MacArthur, *Book on Leadership*; Getz, *Elders and Leaders*; Tozer, *Knowledge of the Holy*; Piper, *Brothers, We Are Not Professionals*; Hughes, *Liberating Ministry*.

Christ).[34] When leaders embody these qualities, they do more than facilitate a study, they inspire transformation.

Discipleship is more "caught" than "taught." Paul reminded Timothy, *"What you have heard from me...entrust to faithful men, who will be able to teach others also"* (2 Timothy 2:2). Leaders multiply disciples and other leaders not by force, but by modeling a life worth imitating. Again, the goal is not perfection but sincerity. Leaders who admit weakness, confess sin, and walk in grace cultivate a culture of growth rather than performance. What flows in you will inevitably flow through you. If you want a healthy, growing, Christ-centered small group, the first place to start is your own heart.

Reflection for Leaders

1. Am I daily rooted in God's Word and prayer?

2. Do I model emotional and spiritual resilience for my group?

3. Am I serving out of humility, or striving out of ambition?

4. Would I want others to imitate my walk with Christ?

---

[34] Blanchard and Hodges, *The Servant Leader*, 23.

Character Check Audit

Use the chart on the following page to honestly assess your character as a small group leader. Pause for a moment in prayer before taking the *Character Check Audit*. If you are unsure how to answer a question, seek guidance from a mentor or an accountability partner. Once you have completed the audit, return to the space provided below and journal your reflections.

_____
_____
_____
_____
_____
_____
_____
_____
_____
_____
_____
_____
_____
_____
_____
_____
_____
_____
_____
_____
_____
_____
_____

Category	Statements to Consider	Often	Sometimes	Rarely/Never
Spiritual Maturity	I spend daily time in prayer and God's Word.			
	My leadership flows from dependence on Christ, not self-effort.			
Integrity	My private life matches my public example.			
	I model what I teach in front of others.			
Humility	I serve others rather than seeking recognition.			
	I confess sin and admit weakness when needed.			
Teachability	I welcome feedback from others without defensiveness.			
	I pursue growth in Christ, not complacency.			
Shepherding Heart	I regularly pray for each member of my group by name.			
	I walk with people in both their joys and struggles.			

Chapter 3: The Framework of Small Group Ministry

"Let us consider how to stir up one another to love and good works, not neglecting to meet together, as is the habit of some, but encouraging one another, and all the more as you see the Day drawing near." — Hebrews 10:24–25 (ESV)

Why a Framework Matters

The New Testament never leaves discipleship to chance. From the beginning, the people of God were given rhythms and patterns to keep them centered on Him. Without those rhythms, God's people always drift. Israel was warned to keep God's Word *"on your heart...teach them diligently to your children... bind them as a sign on your hand"* (Deuteronomy 6:6–8). The early church likewise was marked by devotion, not accident: *"And they devoted themselves to the apostles' teaching and the fellowship, to the breaking of bread and the prayers"* (Acts 2:42, ESV).

Small groups thrive on that kind of clarity. Without a biblical framework, a group can easily tilt too far in one direction, becoming only a Bible class, or only a fellowship gathering, or only a prayer circle. Each element has value, but none alone captures the fullness of discipleship. Paul reminded the Ephesian elders to keep balance, *"I did not shrink from declaring to you anything that was profitable, and teaching you in public and from house to house"* (Acts 20:20).

A framework provides the structure for balance. It ensures that the group keeps its focus on God, builds authentic relationships, and moves outward in mission. Jesus Himself modeled this balance. He went up the mountain to pray to the Father (Luke 6:12), lived in deep community with the Twelve (Mark 3:14), and sent them out to preach and heal (Luke 9:1–2). A group without framework may keep running, but a group with framework will grow in Christ and extend His mission.

The UP–IN–OUT Rhythm

Every healthy small group needs a clear biblical rhythm to guide its life together. Without it, a group may drift into becoming a social club, a therapy circle, or a lecture hall. All of these have a place, but none alone reflect the full mission of the church.

A simple yet powerful way to capture this biblical balance is *The UP–IN–OUT* rhythm:

- **UP (Worship & Word):** Groups seek God together through prayer and Scripture. Jesus declared, *"I am the vine; you are the branches…apart from me you can do nothing"* (John 15:5). Paul commanded Timothy, *"Devote yourself to the public reading of Scripture, to exhortation, to teaching"* (1 Timothy 4:13). Discipleship always begins with seeking God.

- **IN (Community):** Groups build authentic relationships through encouragement, accountability, and care. Hebrews exhorts, *"Let us consider how to stir up one another to love and good works, not neglecting to meet together…but encouraging one another"* (Hebrews 10:24–25). Paul urged the Galatians, *"Bear one another's burdens, and so fulfill the law of Christ"* (Galatians 6:2). Biblical community is not optional; it is commanded.

- **OUT (Mission):** Groups engage the world through service, hospitality, and gospel witness. Jesus told His disciples, *"As the Father has sent me, even so I am sending you"* (John 20:21). The Great Commission calls every believer to *"go therefore and make disciples of all nations"* (Matthew 28:19). And Peter reminds us to *"always be prepared to make a defense…for the hope that is in you"* (1 Peter 3:15).

This rhythm is not a clever model; it is the heartbeat of the New Testament church (Acts 2:42-47). It ensures that groups remain centered on God, strengthened in fellowship, and mobilized for mission.[35] Though simple, this rhythm is comprehensive. It ensures that small groups reflect both the Great Commandment (love God, love others) and the Great Commission (make disciples).

---

[35] Mike Breen and Steve Cockram, *Building a Discipling Culture*, 3rd ed. (Pawleys Island, SC: 3DM Publishing, 2011), 45–52; Jim Putman, *Real-Life Discipleship: Building Churches That Make Disciples* (Colorado Springs: NavPress, 2010), 87–94; Bill Donahue, *Leading Life-Changing Small Groups*, 2nd ed. (Grand Rapids: Zondervan, 2012), 112–18; Dietrich Bonhoeffer, *Life Together* (San Francisco: HarperSanFrancisco, 1954), 25–31; hereafter cited as Breen and Cockram, *BDC*; Putman, *RLD*; Donahue, *Life-Changing Small Groups*; and Bonhoeffer, *Life Together*.

Marks of a Healthy Group

- Worship is central, not optional.
- Relationships are authentic, not superficial.
- Mission is intentional, not accidental.
- Leaders are growing, not coasting.
- Discipleship is multiplying, not stagnating.

The Three Pillars of Purpose

The UP–IN–OUT rhythm finds its clarity when anchored in three biblical pillars: Evangelism, Discipleship, and Fellowship. These are not optional add-ons to the Christian life but essential purposes of the church, flowing from Christ's Great Commission and the early church's example.[36]

1. Evangelism: Reaching the Lost

Small groups are not closed circles but open doors. The gospel itself is outward-focused. Paul declared, *"I am not ashamed of the gospel, for it is the power of God for salvation to everyone who believes"* (Romans 1:16 ESV). Evangelism is not one program among many but the heartbeat of God Himself, who *"desires all people to be saved and to come to the knowledge of the truth"* (1 Timothy 2:4). The New Testament shows that evangelism is the following:

---

[36] Breen and Cockram, *BDC*, 47; Putman, *RLD*, 90; Donahue, *Life-Changing Small Groups*, 115; Bonhoeffer, *Life Together*, 27.

- **Scriptural:** Philip explained the good news to the Ethiopian eunuch directly from Isaiah (Acts 8:35). Paul reasoned from the Scriptures in synagogues (Acts 17:2; 28:23). Evangelism must stay tethered to God's Word, not merely human stories or strategies.

- **Intentional:** Paul set his face toward Rome, eager to preach the gospel (Romans 1:15). The apostles sought opportunities, not waiting passively for the lost to stumble in.

- **Relational:** Evangelism in Acts flowed out of relationships—whether in homes, workplaces, or public gatherings (Acts 2:46–47). As Rosaria Butterfield emphasizes, "radically ordinary hospitality"[37] is often the bridge by which unbelievers experience the love of Christ.

- **Continual:** Disciples make disciples who make disciples. Paul reminded Timothy of his grandmother Lois and his mother Eunice—showing the gospel passed through generations (2 Timothy 1:5).

George Barna's research confirms this intentional relationship method, nearly one-third of unchurched adults say they would attend a small group if personally invited.[38] Evangelism, then, is not abstract. It is a reachable goal, if

---

[37] Rosaria Butterfield, *The Gospel Comes with a House Key: Practicing Radically Ordinary Hospitality in Our Post-Christian World* (Wheaton, IL: Crossway, 2018), 31.

[38] George Barna, *Growing True Disciples: New Strategies for Producing Genuine Followers of Christ* (Colorado Springs: WaterBrook Press, 2001), 109

God's people open their lives, extend invitations, and speak the truth of Christ with grace.

2. Discipleship : Growing in Christ

Jesus' final command was not merely to make converts but disciples: *"teaching them to observe all that I have commanded you"* (Matthew 28:19–20). Discipleship is transformation, not just information. It shapes both character (the fruit of the Spirit, Galatians 5:22–23) and competence (skills in prayer, Scripture, service, and mission).

Ken Braddy reminds leaders that discipleship requires both planning and preparing:

- **Planning** aligns with God's character. As Proverbs teaches, *"Commit your work to the Lord, and your plans will be established"* (Proverbs 16:3). Jesus Himself used planning imagery when He said, *"Which of you, desiring to build a tower, does not first sit down and count the cost?"* (Luke 14:28). Good discipleship does not happen by accident—it requires intentionality.

- **Preparing** means tailoring investment to each person's stage of maturity. Paul discipled Timothy differently than he did Titus. Leaders must discern where people are spiritually and shepherd accordingly.

- **Participating** points to shared life. Jesus discipled His followers not only in sermons but around tables, on roads, and in fields. As Braddy notes, "Some of the best discipleship takes place outside the classroom…it worked pretty well for Jesus, didn't it?"[39]

In a small group framework, discipleship thrives because Scripture is applied in community with accountability, prayer, and encouragement (Hebrews 10:24–25).

3. Fellowship: Life Together

The early church *"devoted themselves to the apostles' teaching and the fellowship"* (Acts 2:42). Fellowship (koinonia) is more than coffee and conversation; it is the shared life of God's people, rooted in Christ. Paul declared, *"You were called into the fellowship of his Son, Jesus Christ our Lord"* (1 Corinthians 1:9).

Fellowship includes the following traits:

- **Praying together:** Prayer is not just individual discipline but a corporate practice. Paul urged the Thessalonians to *"pray without ceasing"* (1 Thessalonians 5:17), and groups today can model this through prayer walks, shared intercession, and praying Scripture.

- **Sharing and caring:** The church in Acts sold possessions to meet needs (Acts 2:44–45). Fellowship means bearing one another's burdens (Galatians 6:2) and practicing hospitality (Romans 12:13). As Dietrich Bonhoeffer

---

[39] Ken Braddy, *Breathing Life into Sunday School: 12 Essentials for Effective Bible Teaching* (Nashville: B&H Publishing, 2019), 47–48

wrote in Life Together, Christian community is a gift of grace that requires intentional service.[40]

- **Serving together:** Groups that serve together embody Christ's teaching: *"By this all people will know that you are my disciples, if you have love for one another"* (John 13:35). Whether through local missions, care packages, or visiting the hurting, fellowship becomes missional.

Fellowship cannot be forced in a single weekly meeting. It is cultivated as believers weave their lives together throughout the week from sharing meals, bearing sorrows, celebrating victories, and walking in holiness.

The Three Pillars of Purpose, Evangelism, Discipleship, and Fellowship, form the biblical framework for small groups. Evangelism opens the door, discipleship strengthens the heart, and fellowship sustains the body. Without this framework, groups drift into imbalance; with it, groups reflect the New Testament vision of the church: a people who reach outward with the gospel, grow upward in Christ, and draw inward to live as the family of God.[41]

Culture Over Meeting

A small group is far more than a calendar slot or a weekly gathering. Groups flourish not merely because of structure, curriculum, or teaching style, but ultimately because of the culture that takes root. Culture drives discipleship more than

---

[40] Dietrich Bonhoeffer, *Life Together*, trans. John W. Doberstein (New York: Harper & Row, 1954), 4 (on Christian fellowship as a gift of grace) and 14 (on service characterized as simple, non-methodical helping love).

[41] Breen and Cockram, *BDC*, 47; Putman, *RLD*, 90; Donahue, *Life-Changing Small Groups*, 115; Bonhoeffer, *Life Together*, 27.

programming. It answers the unspoken question: "What kind of people are we becoming together?"

The Power of Culture

The Bible repeatedly shows that the culture of God's people determines whether they flourish or falter. In the book of Judges, when *"everyone did what was right in his own eyes"* (Judges 21:25), the absence of shared godly culture led to spiritual chaos. By contrast, when the early church devoted themselves to the apostles' teaching, fellowship, breaking bread, and prayers, *"the Lord added to their number day by day those who were being saved"* (Acts 2:42, 47). Culture is not accidental, it is cultivated. Leaders shape culture by four habits:[42]

- **Celebrate:** Barnabas *"saw the grace of God, and he was glad"* (Acts 11:23). What groups choose to celebrate—spiritual growth or mere attendance, transformation or just tradition, will be repeated.

---

[42] Edmund P. Clowney, *The Church* (Contours of Christian Theology; Downers Grove, IL: InterVarsity Press, 1995), 207–12; Colin Marshall and Tony Payne, *The Trellis and the Vine: The Ministry Mind-Shift That Changes Everything* (Kingsford, Australia: Matthias Media, 2009), 37–46; Jim Putman, Bobby Harrington, and Robert Coleman, *DiscipleShift: Five Steps That Help Your Church to Make Disciples Who Make Disciples* (Grand Rapids: Zondervan, 2013), 75–88; Mike Breen and Steve Cockram, *Building a Discipling Culture* (3rd ed.; Pawleys Island, SC: 3DM Publishing, 2011), 113–28; Eric Geiger and Kevin Peck, *Designed to Lead: The Church and Leadership Development* (Nashville: B&H, 2016), 94–105; Brandon Guindon, *Disciple-Making Culture: Cultivate Thriving Disciple-Makers by Using the Five Elements of a Disciple-Making Culture* (Exponential, 2020), 51–64.

- **Repeat:** Hebrews 10:24–25 exhorts believers to *"stir up one another to love and good works"* by not neglecting to meet together. The practices a group repeats, such as praying, encouraging, and serving, become its rhythms.

- **Remember:** Israel was commanded to retell God's works (Deuteronomy 6:4–9; Psalm 78:4). Small groups that recall answered prayers, life-change stories, and God's faithfulness form a gospel-centered memory.

- **Model:** Paul told the Corinthians, *"Be imitators of me, as I am of Christ"* (1 Corinthians 11:1). What leaders live out—hospitality, humility, integrity—sets the tone for the group.

Marks of a Gospel-Shaped Culture

A healthy small group culture does not emerge by accident; it takes shape when the gospel becomes the guiding influence for how the group lives, prays, cares, celebrates, and serves together. The framework of *UP–IN–OUT*, looking upward to God, inward to one another, and outward to the world, must move beyond being a catchy phrase and become the instinctive rhythm of the group's life. When this happens, the group reflects not just good organization but the very heartbeat of the gospel.

In a gospel-shaped culture, **prayer becomes natural, not forced.** The early church was marked by persistent prayer (Acts 1:14; 4:31), showing us that prayer is not simply a filler between activities but the very atmosphere in which discipleship grows. A healthy group breathes prayer. it is woven into conversations, decisions, and relationships, creating a space where God's presence is constantly acknowledged and depended upon.

A gospel-shaped culture also means that **care is shared, not left to one person.** Paul's image of the church as a body reminds us that when one member suffers, all suffer together (1 Corinthians 12:26). Small groups thrive when burdens are carried collectively, not placed solely on the leader. This shared care creates a sense of belonging and safety, where members know they are not alone but are surrounded by brothers and sisters committed to walking with them.

Another key element is that **stories of God's work are celebrated and retold.** The psalmist declared, *"One generation shall commend your works to another"* (Psalm 145:4). Testimonies of God's faithfulness strengthen the group's faith and set an expectation that God is actively working in their lives. When stories are shared and celebrated, hope rises, gratitude deepens, and members are reminded that their faith is part of a larger story of God's ongoing mission.

Finally, in a gospel-shaped culture, **service is expected, not optional**. Jesus washed His disciples' feet and commanded them to follow His example (John 13:14–15). A small group shaped by the gospel does not exist for itself; it exists to serve together in the church and the community. Service redirects the group outward, preventing it from becoming insular or self-focused. When groups serve side by side, they embody Christ's humility, extend His love, and show the watching world what the gospel looks like in action.[43]

Questions Every Group Should Ask

Culture can drift inward or outward, gospel-centered or clique-centered. Left unchecked, the direction of a group's culture will shape its identity more than its intentions. Every small group should ask:

- Do we have a gospel-centered culture where God's Word, prayer, and mission are central (Acts 2:42-47)?

- Do we have a mission-focused culture that seeks the lost and serves the community (Matthew 28:19-20)?

- Do we have a hospitality culture where outsiders feel welcomed (Romans 15:7)?

- Have we slipped into a comfort culture, just a social club or clique where only insiders belong?

The culture of your small group will either propel or paralyze its mission. Curriculum may guide lessons, but culture shapes lives. When a group lives out the framework of evangelism, discipleship, and fellowship with prayer, care, story, and service at its core, it becomes not just a meeting but

---

[43] Clowney, *The Church*, 207–12; Marshall and Payne, *Trellis and Vine*, 37–46; Putman, Harrington, and Coleman, *DiscipleShift*, 75–88; Breen and Cockram, *Building a Discipling Culture*, 113–28; Geiger and Peck, *Designed to Lead*, 94–105; Guindon, *Disciple-Making Culture*, 51–64.

a movement.[44] Additional small group resources on building culture are provided in Appendices 1–3.

The End Goal: Multiplication

The framework is not complete unless it reproduces. Small groups are never meant to be spiritual cul-de-sacs where blessing ends; they are to be gospel highways where life and mission flow outward. From Genesis to Revelation, God's design for His people is multiplication: *"Be fruitful and multiply and fill the earth"* (Genesis 1:28). This mandate, first physical, becomes spiritual in Christ: *"Go therefore and make disciples of all nations"* (Matthew 28:19).

Paul's charge to Timothy makes the principle unmistakable, *"What you have heard from me in the presence of many witnesses entrust to faithful men, who will be able to teach others also"* (2 Timothy 2:2). This is four generations of multiplication in a single verse: Paul → Timothy → faithful men → others. The gospel message is not just taught; it is transformative.[45]

---

[44] Clowney, *The Church*, 207–12; Marshall and Payne, *Trellis and Vine*, 37–46; Putman, Harrington, and Coleman, *DiscipleShift*, 75–88; Breen and Cockram, *Building a Discipling Culture*, 113–28; Geiger and Peck, *Designed to Lead*, 94–105; Guindon, *Disciple-Making Culture*, 51–64.

[45] Robert E. Coleman, *The Master Plan of Evangelism* (2nd ed.; Grand Rapids: Revell, 1993), 89–102; Bill Hull, *The Disciple-Making Pastor: Leading Others on the Journey of Faith* (rev. ed.; Grand Rapids: Baker, 2007), 145–59; Jim Putman and Bobby Harrington, *Discipleshift: Five Steps That Help Your Church to Make Disciples Who Make Disciples* (Grand Rapids: Zondervan, 2013), 121–37; Steve Timmis and Tim Chester, *Total Church: A Radical Reshaping around Gospel and Community* (Wheaton, IL: Crossway, 2008), 117–29; Brandon Guindon, *Disciple-Making Culture: Cultivate Thriving Disciple-Makers by Using the Five Elements of a Disciple-Making Culture* (Exponential, 2020), 95–112; Mike Breen and Steve Cockram, *Building a Discipling Culture* (3rd ed.; Pawleys Island, SC: 3DM Publishing, 2011), 185–201.

Multiplication vs. Maintenance

Too many groups settle into maintenance mode, comfortable circles where insiders are fed but outsiders are forgotten. But disciples are not made to sit; they are made to send. We were not saved to hide but to herald (Romans 10:14–15). A group that only looks inward loses sight of its mission. Multiplication means the following actions:

- **Reproducing disciples:** Jesus called fishermen and said, *"Follow me, and I will make you fishers of men"* (Matthew 4:19). His call was never to stagnation but to reproduction.

- **Reproducing leaders:** Barnabas brought Saul into ministry (Acts 11:25–26), then later gave John Mark a second chance (Acts 15:37–39). Leaders reproduce leaders by opening doors and equipping others.

- **Reproducing groups:** The church in Antioch multiplied missionaries (Acts 13:1–3), sending out Paul and Barnabas. Healthy groups should not cling to growth for the sake of pride but release people for the sake of mission.[46]

Barriers to Multiplication

The greatest obstacles to multiplication are often not logistical but spiritual. Leaders must remain on guard against common barriers that hinder multiplication. These challenges

---

[46] Coleman, *Master Plan of Evangelism*, 89–102; Hull, *Disciple-Making Pastor*, 145–59; Putman and Harrington, *Discipleshift*, 121–37; Timmis and Chester, *Total Church*, 117–29; Guindon, *Disciple-Making Culture*, 95–112; Breen and Cockram, *Building a Discipling Culture*, 185–201.

are subtle, but they can easily stall growth if left unchecked. By identifying and addressing them early, leaders can keep their groups focused on the mission of making disciples.

- **Pride:** Leaders who cling to control or recognition hinder the raising of others. John the Baptist gives the right model, *"He must increase, but I must decrease"* (John 3:30).

- **Comfort:** A desire to keep the same familiar circle resists the outward push of the gospel. Yet Jesus broke His disciples out of comfort zones, sending them from Jerusalem to Judea, Samaria, and the ends of the earth (Acts 1:8).

- **Fear:** Leaders sometimes fear losing quality if they release others. But the Holy Spirit, not human ability, empowers multiplication (Acts 1:8; 1 Corinthians 2:4–5).[47]

A Framework That Reproduce

A strong small group framework will always lead toward multiplication—not for the sake of numbers, but for the sake of people encountering Christ. Multiplication is the natural outcome of gospel-centered culture:

- As evangelism is practiced, **new believers are added**.
- As discipleship deepens, **new leaders are raised**.
- As fellowship grows, **new groups are formed**.

---

[47] Coleman, *Master Plan of Evangelism*, 89–102; Hull, *Disciple-Making Pastor*, 145–59; Putman and Harrington, *Discipleshift*, 121–37; Timmis and Chester, *Total Church*, 117–29; Guindon, *Disciple-Making Culture*, 95–112; Breen and Cockram, *Building a Discipling Culture*, 185–201.

Healthy small groups become incubators for disciple-makers and launching pads for new leaders. When leaders see themselves not as the end but as the means—entrusting the gospel to others—they fulfill Christ's design for His church. We are not called to isolation, pride, or ego-stroking. We are called to reproduce. The true test of a small group's health is not how many attend, but how many are sent. The framework of *UP–IN–OUT* reaches its God-given goal only when disciples multiply disciples, leaders multiply leaders, and groups multiply groups—until the whole world hears the good news of Jesus Christ.[48]

Reflective Questions

1. Does my group consistently reflect the UP–IN–OUT rhythm?

2. Which of the three pillars—evangelism, discipleship, fellowship—needs strengthening in my group?

3. Am I shaping culture beyond the meeting, or only running meetings?

4. Who in my group could be an apprentice leader to carry the mission forward?

---

[48] Coleman, *Master Plan of Evangelism*, 89–102; Hull, *Disciple-Making Pastor*, 145–59; Putman and Harrington, *Discipleshift*, 121–37; Timmis and Chester, *Total Church*, 117–29; Guindon, *Disciple-Making Culture*, 95–112; Breen and Cockram, *Building a Discipling Culture*, 185–201.

Conclusion to Part 1: Foundations

The foundation of small group ministry is built on Scripture, shaped by godly leaders, and guided by a disciple-making framework. Without these anchors, small groups can easily drift into becoming little more than social gatherings, activity clubs, or even theological discussion circles with no real-life impact. But when they are grounded in the Word, led by Christlike shepherds, and directed by the mission of making disciples, small groups become far more than meetings on a calendar—they become the very heartbeat of the church's life and witness.

The book of Acts shows us that the early church gathered not only in the temple courts but also from house to house, *"devoted…to the apostles' teaching and the fellowship, to the breaking of bread and the prayers"* (Acts 2:42). This rhythm of worship, community, and mission is still the biblical blueprint for today. Healthy groups grow because they are nourished by God's Word. They thrive because leaders model integrity, humility, and love. And they multiply because their purpose is not inward comfort but outward commission—to make disciples who make disciples.

Ultimately, the purpose of small groups is nothing less than participating in the Great Commission. Jesus commanded His disciples to *"go…make disciples of all nations…teaching them to observe all that I have commanded you"* (Matthew 28:19–20). Small groups provide the relational context where that teaching, training, and transformation happen most naturally. They are the furnace where faith is refined, the table where fellowship is deepened, and the launching pad where mission is carried forward.

As we move into Part Two—Principles for Leading Small Groups, keep in mind that a strong foundation is only the beginning. A house with solid footings must still be built up, room by room. In the same way, a small group ministry built on biblical truth, godly leadership, and clear purpose must now be equipped with practical tools, rhythms, and strategies for fruitfulness. With these foundations in place, we are ready to explore how to lead groups that not only gather, but grow, and ultimately go for the glory of God.

Part 2: Principles

Chapter 4: Preparation

"Do your best to present yourself to God as one approved, a worker who has no need to be ashamed, rightly handling the word of truth." – 2 Timothy 2:15 (ESV)

Every thriving small group begins long before the first person walks into the room. Leadership rises and falls on preparation. When leaders neglect it, groups drift into mediocrity. But when leaders prepare well, groups become life-giving communities where discipleship flourishes. Preparation has three inseparable layers: preparing yourself, preparing the Word, and preparing the environment. Each is essential, and together they provide fertile ground for the Spirit of God to work.

Why Preparation Matters

No builder begins construction without a blueprint. No farmer plants without first preparing the soil. In the same way, no small group leader should enter a gathering without careful preparation. Preparation is more than reviewing curriculum; it is the spiritual, mental, and practical readiness of the leader.

Again, Harrington Emerson's timeless maxim captures this well, "Methods are many. Principles are few. Methods always change. Principles never do."[49] Preparation is one of those timeless principles. A leader who fails to prepare not only weakens the teaching but also risks missing opportunities for God to work through the group.

---

[49] Harrington Emerson, *Twelve Principles of Efficiency* (New York: The Engineering Magazine, 1912), 17.

The apostle Paul exhorted Timothy to *"rightly handle the word of truth"* (2 Timothy 2:15). This responsibility is both sacred and serious. Leaders prepare not simply to manage a meeting but to shepherd souls.[50]

Common Pitfalls in Preparation

While preparation is essential, many small group leaders stumble into avoidable mistakes. Some prepare too little, arriving with only a quick skim of the passage. This often results in shallow conversation or awkward silences. Others prepare too much, packing their notes so tightly that the meeting becomes a lecture rather than a discussion. Another common pitfall is relying only on curriculum, treating the guide as a script instead of a resource. Most serious of all, some leaders skip prayer entirely, preparing their minds while neglecting their hearts.

Let's be honest—every one of us has fallen into these pitfalls at some point. I know that I have. I've prepared a lesson the night before, I've made sessions more about lectures than discussion, and I've entered a study without preparing my own heart before the Lord. These are not just abstract warnings;

---

[50] See Steve Gladen, *Planning Small Groups with Purpose: A Field-Tested Guide to Design and Grow Your Ministry* (Grand Rapids: Baker, 2018), 41–63; Andy Stanley and Bill Willits, *Creating Community: Five Keys to Building a Small Group Culture* (Colorado Springs: Multnomah, 2004), 75–101; Bill Donahue and Russ Robinson, *Building a Church of Small Groups: A Place Where Nobody Stands Alone* (Grand Rapids: Zondervan, 2001), 134–49; Jim Putman, *Real-Life Discipleship: Building Churches That Make Disciples* (Colorado Springs: NavPress, 2010), 89–112; Brandon Guindon, *Disciple-Making Culture: Cultivate Thriving Disciple-Makers Throughout Your Church* (Colorado Springs: NavPress, 2020), 147–66; Mike Breen, *Building a Discipling Culture* (3rd ed.; Pawleys Island, SC: 3DM Publishing, 2017), 91–110; Spence Shelton, "Preparing Leaders for Missional Small Groups," *Journal of Discipleship and Family Ministry* 2.2 (2012): 24–37.

they are lived realities for many of us. In over twenty-seven years of ministry, I've seen countless small group leaders wait until the night before—or even just hours before—their group to begin preparing. Sadly, this has become more common than rare. But God's Word deserves more, and our people deserve more. We are called to be disciples who make disciples, and the truth is that we reproduce what we are.[51]

The writer of Proverbs reminds us that *"the plans of the diligent lead surely to abundance"* (Proverbs 21:5). True diligence is more than content mastery; it is prayerful, Spirit-dependent, and people-oriented. Avoiding these pitfalls keeps preparation both faithful and fruitful.

The Three Layers of Preparation

Layer 1 — Preparing Yourself: Spiritual Readiness

Small group leadership begins in the leader's soul. Before a leader prepares notes or arranges chairs, they must first come before the Lord in humility. Prayer, repentance, and dependence on the Spirit form the unseen foundation of effective leadership. These themes—introduced in greater detail in Chapter 2 on the character of the leader—remind us that spiritual preparation is the starting point for every healthy group.

Acts 11:24 describes Barnabas as *"a good man, full of the Holy Spirit and of faith."* His leadership influence did not come from charisma, but from Spirit-filled character. Small group leaders must likewise prepare their hearts through:

---

[51] Jim Putman, *Real-Life Discipleship: Building Churches That Make Disciples* (Colorado Springs: NavPress, 2010), 43

- **Personal Holiness:** Keeping short accounts with God through confession and repentance (1 John 1:9).

- **Prayerful Intercession:** Lifting group members and their needs before the Lord (Ephesians 6:18).

- **Posture of Dependence on the Spirit:** Acknowledging that true change comes only through His power (Zechariah 4:6).

J.R. Miller wisely noted that "power in ministry comes from the leader's own spiritual life."[52] A prayerless leader may impart information, but a praying leader imparts transformation.[53]

Layer 2 — Preparing the Word: Study Methods and Resources

Once the leader's heart is postured toward God, preparation turns to His Word. Small group leadership is not about filling time or sparking casual discussion, it is about opening Scripture so that lives are changed. God's Word is living and active (Hebrews 4:12), and when faithfully studied and taught, it pierces hearts, renews minds, and shapes disciples into Christlikeness. Leaders are not entertainers but stewards of Scripture, entrusted with the responsibility to handle it with reverence and clarity (2 Timothy 2:15). This sacred trust calls

[52] J.R. Miller, The Building of Character (New York: Thomas Y. Crowell, 1909), 45

[53] See Gladen, *Planning Small Groups with Purpose*, 41–63; Stanley and Willits, *Creating Community*, 75–101; Donahue and Robinson, Building a Church of Small Groups, 134–49; Putman, *Real-Life Discipleship*, 89–112; Guindon, *Disciple-Making Culture*, 147–66; Breen, *Building a Discipling Culture*, 91–110; Shelton, "Preparing Leaders for Missional Small Groups," 24–37.

leaders to prepare well, because through the Word God speaks, convicts, and transforms. Sound preparation follows three steps:

1. **Perceive the Text: What do I see in the text?**
Observation of the text begins with careful reading. Who wrote the passage? Who was the audience? What are the key words, repeated themes, and historical context? As Gordon Fee and Douglas Stuart remind us, "To make a text mean something God did not intend is to abuse the text, not use it."[54]

2. **Process the Text: What does the text mean?**
Interpretation asks: What did this mean to the original audience? What does it reveal about God and about humanity? What promises, commands, or warnings are present? Biblical hermeneutics ensures we hear the text in its context, guided by the Spirit.

3. **Practice the Text: How should this change me (and us)?**
Application moves from head to heart to hands. How should we live differently because of this passage? What is the text calling us to do? How does it shape our relationships with God and others? Paul reminded Timothy that all Scripture is *"breathed out by God and profitable for teaching, for reproof, for correction, and for training in righteousness"* (2 Timothy 3:16–17).

Leaders who skip observation and interpretation and rush straight to application risk misusing Scripture. When leaders

---

[54] Gordon D. Fee and Douglas Stuart, How to Read the Bible for All Its Worth, 4th ed. (Grand Rapids: Zondervan, 2014), 29.

perceive, process, and practice the Word, they handle Scripture faithfully and lead their groups toward lasting transformation.

Preparing with Tools: Resources for Study

God's Word is sufficient, but He has also provided tools to help us understand it. Fee suggests three essentials for every student of Scripture:[55]

- **A good translation of the Bible,** which will be an accurate and readable rendering of the original text.

- **A good Bible dictionary,** which provides definitions and explanations of biblical words, places, and concepts.

- **Good commentaries,** which offer verse-by-verse explanations and insights from biblical scholars.

Other helpful resources that I would include:

- **Bible Handbook,** which gives an overview and background of each book of the Bible.

- **Concordance,** which offers word studies, to help you dive deeper into the original langue and intent.

- **Topical Bible,** which explores subjects and themes throughout the Bible.

- **Study Apps** (Logos, Blue Letter Bible, Bible Gateway).

----

[55] Fee and Stuart, How to Read the Bible, 33.

Ken Braddy reminds leaders that curriculum is "a guide, not a script."[56] Leaders should internalize the text, not simply read questions off a page. Good preparation allows the leader to guide discussion with confidence and humility.

A Weekly Prep Rhythm

Preparation is not something that happens all at once the night before group. It is best when spread out, giving the Word time to soak into the leader's own life. A simple weekly rhythm might look like this:

- **Monday:** Read the passage devotionally, asking, "Lord, what are You showing me?"

- **Tuesday–Wednesday:** Study deeper with a commentary, dictionary, or handbook. Write notes and key insights.

- **Thursday–Friday:** Draft questions and think about discussion flow. Pray for each group member by name.

- **Saturday:** Review notes briefly, then rest and trust God.

- **Sunday (or meeting day):** Enter the gathering with expectation, depending on the Spirit to work.

This rhythm models Psalm 1:2, describing the blessed man whose *"delight is in the law of the Lord, and on his law he meditates day and night."*

---

[56] Ken Braddy, Breathing Life into Sunday School: 12 Simple Steps to Increase Attendance and Make Disciples (Nashville: LifeWay, 2019), 57.

Preparing for Discussion: Asking Good Questions

One of the leader's greatest tools is not having all the answers but asking the right questions. Jesus Himself often taught by asking questions that invited reflection (Matthew 16:15). Good questions open the door for the Spirit to speak through Scripture and through one another.[57]

A balanced small group study requires more than just reading a passage together; it requires asking the right kinds of questions. In fact, three types of questions provide the framework for meaningful and transformative discussions. Each plays a distinct role in helping members move from simply hearing the Word to truly living it out, and together they form a rhythm of study that ensures depth, clarity, and personal impact. This subject is explored in greater detail in Chapter 5, but the overview here provides a starting point for leaders to shape their discussions wisely.

The first type is **observation questions**, which focus on what the text says. These questions invite the group to slow down and pay attention to details they might otherwise overlook. For example, asking, 'What repeated words stand out in this passage?' helps participants notice themes, key terms, and patterns. Observation grounds the discussion in Scripture itself, ensuring that interpretation and application are rooted in what the text actually communicates rather than assumptions or personal opinion.

---

[57] See Gladen, *Planning Small Groups with Purpose*, 41–63; Stanley and Willits, *Creating Community*, 75–101; Donahue and Robinson, Building a Church of Small Groups, 134–49; Putman, *Real-Life Discipleship*, 89–112; Guindon, *Disciple-Making Culture*, 147–66; Breen, *Building a Discipling Culture*, 91–110; Shelton, "Preparing Leaders for Missional Small Groups," 24–37.

The second type is **interpretation questions**, which explore what the text means. Observation lays the foundation, but interpretation builds on it by drawing out the author's intent and theological significance. A leader might ask, "Why do you think Paul emphasized faith over works here?" Such questions push members to wrestle with context, meaning, and the bigger picture of God's story. Interpretation questions prevent the group from treating Scripture superficially and instead guide them into deeper understanding.

The third type is **application questions**, which ask how the text should change us. Scripture is not just for knowledge but for transformation, and application questions move the group from insight to obedience. For instance, a leader might ask, "What is one step we can take this week to obey this command?" These questions personalize the message, challenge group members to take practical steps of faith, and remind everyone that discipleship involves both hearing and doing the Word.

Together, observation, interpretation, and application questions form a healthy balance for group study. Without observation, groups risk missing the details of the text; without interpretation, they risk misunderstanding its meaning; without application, they risk failing to live it out. But when all three are present, small groups not only study God's Word, they are shaped by it.

Poorly worded questions, such as yes/no queries ("Do you agree with this verse?") or ones detached from the text ("What do you think about this topic?"), can stall discussion. Strong, open-ended, text-rooted questions move the group from information to transformation.

Layer 3 — Preparing the Environment: Space, Schedule, and Standards

The third layer of preparation involves the physical and relational environment of the group. A cluttered, cold, or distracting room communicates disinterest. A warm, orderly, and welcoming space says, "You matter." This is explored in greater detail in Chapter 9.

- **Space:** Arrange chairs in a circle to foster discussion rather than rows that imply lecture.

- **Schedule:** Begin and end on time, respecting members' commitments (Matthew 5:37).

- **Standards:** Clarify group values such as confidentiality, participation, and accountability (Romans 12:10).[58]

As Braddy also reminds us, planning is "a God thing."[59] Proverbs 16:3 says, *"Commit your work to the Lord, and your plans will be established."* Preparation is an act of stewardship, aligning our efforts with God's purposes.

---

[58] See Gladen, *Planning Small Groups with Purpose*, 41–63; Stanley and Willits, *Creating Community*, 75–101; Donahue and Robinson, Building a Church of Small Groups, 134–49; Putman, *Real-Life Discipleship*, 89–112; Guindon, *Disciple-Making Culture*, 147–66; Breen, *Building a Discipling Culture*, 91–110; Shelton, "Preparing Leaders for Missional Small Groups," 24–37.

[59] Ken Braddy, "Planning Is a God Thing," Ken Braddy Blog, accessed August 22, 2025, https://kenbraddy.com.

Small Group Prep Checklist

- Have I prayed for my group?
- Have I studied the passage deeply?
- Is the room prepared and welcoming?
- Do members know the time and place?
- Do I expect God to move?

Preparing Relationally: Knowing Your People

Preparation also includes preparing to love the people God has entrusted to you. Jesus said, *"I am the good shepherd. I know my own and my own know me"* (John 10:14). A shepherd cannot lead sheep he does not know, and a small group leader cannot effectively disciple people without understanding their lives, struggles, and joys.

Relational preparation may look like:

- **Learning their stories:** Take time to ask about members' backgrounds, testimonies, and spiritual journeys.

- **Praying specifically:** Keep a prayer journal with names, needs, and answered prayers. Paul modeled this when he told the Colossians, *"we have not ceased to pray for you"* (Colossians 1:9).

- **Following up with care:** A quick text, coffee, or word of encouragement during the week communicates that you value people beyond the meeting.

A well-prepared leader enters the group not only with notes on the passage but also with names and needs written on their heart.[60]

Preparing for Challenges: Handling Disruptions

Even with the best preparation, leaders will face challenges in the group setting. The enemy delights in distraction, division, and discouragement. Wise leaders prepare for these moments in advance.[61] Chapter 13 explores this subject in greater detail.

- **When one person dominates:** Affirm their eagerness but gently redirect: "That's a great point—let's hear from someone who hasn't shared yet."

- **When no one speaks:** Don't panic. Re-ask the question more simply, share a personal insight, or give a moment of silence for reflection. Remember silence is not our enemy.

- **When error arises:** Correct gently, pointing back to Scripture: "That's an interesting thought. Let's look at what Paul actually says in verse 12." (Ephesians 4:15).

---

[60] See Gladen, *Planning Small Groups with Purpose*, 41–63; Stanley and Willits, *Creating Community*, 75–101; Donahue and Robinson, Building a Church of Small Groups, 134–49; Putman, *Real-Life Discipleship*, 89–112; Guindon, *Disciple-Making Culture*, 147–66; Breen, *Building a Discipling Culture*, 91–110; Shelton, "Preparing Leaders for Missional Small Groups," 24–37.

[61] See Gladen, *Planning Small Groups with Purpose*, 41–63; Stanley and Willits, *Creating Community*, 75–101; Donahue and Robinson, Building a Church of Small Groups, 134–49; Putman, *Real-Life Discipleship*, 89–112; Guindon, *Disciple-Making Culture*, 147–66; Breen, *Building a Discipling Culture*, 91–110; Shelton, "Preparing Leaders for Missional Small Groups," 24–37.

- **When sensitive issues surface:** Handle with compassion, reminding the group of confidentiality and offering to follow up privately if needed.

Colossians 4:6 reminds leaders, *"Let your speech always be gracious, seasoned with salt."* A prepared leader expects disruptions but leans on the Spirit to turn challenges into growth moments.

The Cost of Neglecting Preparation

Neglecting preparation does more than create an unpolished meeting, it shapes the culture of the group and the disciples it produces. A leader who consistently arrives unprepared communicates, even unintentionally, that God's Word is secondary and that people's time is expendable. Over time, this erodes trust and lowers expectations. Members may stop coming ready to engage because they assume little will be required of them.

Theologically, neglect of preparation undermines the sacred charge given to leaders. Paul commanded Timothy to "do your best to present yourself to God as one approved… rightly handling the word of truth" (2 Timothy 2:15). Mishandling or under-handling Scripture not only risks error but fails to honor the God who speaks through His Word. Neglect becomes not just a practical issue but a spiritual one— a matter of stewardship.

Relationally, when leaders fail to prepare, groups tend to drift toward shallowness. Prayer becomes rushed, discussion becomes surface-level, and fellowship remains polite but not transformative. Without a leader modeling diligence, members learn to settle for mediocrity in their own walk with Christ. We reproduce what we are, and unprepared leaders tend to form unprepared disciples.

The Scriptures give us a sharp contrast in the example of Ezra. Ezra 7:10 says, *"For Ezra had set his heart to study the Law of the Lord, and to do it and to teach his statutes and rules in Israel."* Ezra's influence flowed not from charisma or position, but from careful preparation rooted in devotion to God's Word. He studied it personally, applied it obediently, and then taught it faithfully. This threefold pattern—study, obedience, teaching—remains a model for every small group leader today. Neglect, by contrast, produces the opposite: shallow study, inconsistent obedience, and ineffective teaching.[62]

Practically, the long-term cost is multiplication without depth. If future leaders are raised in a culture of hasty, last-minute preparation, then that approach becomes the norm. Instead of building a disciple-making movement rooted in God's Word, churches risk creating gatherings of good intentions without lasting fruit.

Proverbs 21:5 reminds us that *"the plans of the diligent lead surely to abundance, but everyone who is hasty comes only to poverty."* The fruitfulness of a small group is rarely accidental; it is usually the harvest of faithful, prayerful, and Spirit-led preparation. To neglect this work is to accept barrenness where God intends abundance.[63]

---

[62] ESV Study Bible, ed. Wayne Grudem (Wheaton: Crossway, 2008), 798.

[63] See Gladen, *Planning Small Groups with Purpose*, 41–63; Stanley and Willits, *Creating Community*, 75–101; Donahue and Robinson, Building a Church of Small Groups, 134–49; Putman, *Real-Life Discipleship*, 89–112; Guindon, *Disciple-Making Culture*, 147–66; Breen, *Building a Discipling Culture*, 91–110; Shelton, "Preparing Leaders for Missional Small Groups," 24–37.

Preparing for Multiplication

Finally, preparation is not only about leading well this week, it is also about raising up future leaders. Paul told Timothy, *"what you have heard from me in the presence of many witnesses entrust to faithful men, who will be able to teach others also"* (2 Timothy 2:2). Every leader should have an eye toward multiplication. Practical steps for preparing with multiplication in mind include:

- **Identify an apprentice leader:** Find someone faithful, available, and teachable.

- **Involve them in preparation:** Invite them to help draft questions or lead prayer.

- **Debrief after meetings:** Talk through with them what went well and what could improve.

- **Gradually release responsibility:** Allow them to lead a portion of discussion until they can eventually lead a group themselves.

Multiplication keeps groups from stagnating and ensures that disciple-making continues beyond one leader. Leaders prepare not just for the moment but for the mission.[64]

---

[64] See Gladen, *Planning Small Groups with Purpose*, 41–63; Stanley and Willits, *Creating Community*, 75–101; Donahue and Robinson, Building a Church of Small Groups, 134–49; Putman, *Real-Life Discipleship*, 89–112; Guindon, *Disciple-Making Culture*, 147–66; Breen, *Building a Discipling Culture*, 91–110; Shelton, "Preparing Leaders for Missional Small Groups," 24–37.

Conclusion

Preparation is not about perfection but about faithfulness. When leaders prepare themselves, the Word, and the environment, they create the conditions where discipleship thrives and the Spirit of God brings transformation. Preparation also shows small groups that both the leadership of the church and the leader of the group genuinely cares. Just as we would never want to enter an operating room without the surgeon being properly prepared, neither should we enter a small group class where the leader is unprepared.

Reflective Questions

1. Do I begin preparation with prayer and the Word, or do I rush to logistics?

2. Am I equipping myself with sound study tools?

3. Do I know the personal needs of my group members, and have I prayed for them by name this week?

4. Am I training someone else through my preparation process?

5. Did I spend more time preparing my heart than arranging my notes?

Chapter 5: Presentation

"And beginning with Moses and all the Prophets, he interpreted to them in all the Scriptures the things concerning himself." – Luke 24:27 (ESV)

Preparation sets the stage, but presentation brings it to life. Small group leaders are not lecturers delivering monologues but facilitators guiding conversation. Effective presentation combines clarity, humility, and Holy Spirit-led flexibility.

Why Presentation Matters

Preparation without presentation is like planting seeds and never watering them. You may have studied deeply, prayed earnestly, and planned carefully—but how you communicate the Word in the group setting will determine whether people truly grasp and apply it.

Presentation is not about performance. It is about clarity, conviction, and connection. Small group leaders are not professional speakers; they are shepherds guiding conversation around the living Word of God. As Paul reminded the Corinthians, *"My speech and my message were not in plausible words of wisdom, but in demonstration of the Spirit and of power"* (1 Corinthians 2:4). Good presentation does not rely on charisma but on the Spirit working through a prepared servant.[65]

The Shepherding Role in Presentation

Small group leaders are not lecturers behind a podium but shepherds among the flock. Peter exhorted leaders, *"Shepherd the flock of God that is among you, exercising oversight, not under compulsion, but willingly, as God would have you; not for shameful gain, but eagerly"* (1 Peter 5:2). Presentation, then, is an act of shepherding. A shepherd feeds, guides, and protects. In the group context, that means:

- **Feeding:** Presenting the Word of God clearly and nourishing souls with biblical truth (Nehemiah 8:8).

- **Guiding:** Asking questions that point people toward obedience and application (Psalm 23:3).

- **Protecting:** Correcting error and gently steering conversation back to the truth (Acts 20:28–30).

---

[65] See Bill Donahue, *Leading Life-Changing Small Groups* (3rd ed.; Grand Rapids: Zondervan, 2012), 57–82; Steve Gladen, *Small Groups with Purpose: How to Create Healthy Communities* (Grand Rapids: Baker, 2011), 115–36; Andy Stanley, Bill Willits, and Heather Zempel, *Creating Community: Five Keys to Building a Small Group Culture* (rev. ed.; Grand Rapids: Zondervan, 2021), 121–43; Greg Bowman and Bill Donahue, *Coaching Life-Changing Small Group Leaders: A Comprehensive Guide for Developing Leaders of Groups and Teams* (Downers Grove, IL: InterVarsity Press, 2006), 98–112; Trevor Joy and Spence Shelton, *The People of God: Empowering the Church to Make Disciples* (Nashville: B&H, 2014), 85–104; Brandon Guindon, *Disciple-Making Culture: Cultivate Thriving Disciple-Makers Throughout Your Church* (Colorado Springs: NavPress, 2020), 167–88; Reid Smith, "Essentials for Effective Small Group Facilitation," *Christian Education Journal* 12.2 (2015): 221–35.

Presentation is not performance; it is shepherding God's people in the living Word. Leaders who understand their shepherding role will present with patience, gentleness, and conviction.[66]

Creating the Right Atmosphere

The first task of presentation is not words, but atmosphere. Before anyone opens a Bible or answers a question, the feel of the group sets the tone. People must sense that they are safe enough to open up and engaged enough to stay involved. A small group thrives when trust and welcome are woven into the environment.[67] Here are six areas for creating the right atmosphere in a small group:

1. Courtesy is Shown: Courtesy sets the foundation for a healthy small group environment. Members must learn to consider others by listening attentively and without interruption. Leaders should model humility, confessing that they too are learners in the journey of faith. This communicates that no one has "arrived," and every person is still growing in Christ. A courteous tone signals that every member's contribution matters, reinforcing James 1:19, which reminds us to be *"quick to hear, slow to speak, slow to anger."* When

---

[66] See Donahue, *Leading Life-Changing Small Groups*, 57–82; Gladen, *Small Groups with Purpose*, 115–36; Stanley, Willits, and Zempel, *Creating Community*, 121–43; Bowman and Donahue, *Coaching Life-Changing Small Group Leaders*, 98–112; Joy and Shelton, *The People of God*, 85–104; Guindon, *Disciple-Making Culture*, 167–88; Smith, "Essentials for Effective Small Group Facilitation," 221–35.

[67] See Donahue, *Leading Life-Changing Small Groups*, 57–82; Gladen, *Small Groups with Purpose*, 115–36; Stanley, Willits, and Zempel, *Creating Community*, 121–43; Bowman and Donahue, *Coaching Life-Changing Small Group Leaders*, 98–112; Joy and Shelton, *The People of God*, 85–104; Guindon, *Disciple-Making Culture*, 167–88; Smith, "Essentials for Effective Small Group Facilitation," 221–35.

courtesy is shown, members feel valued, respected, and free to participate fully.

2. Conversation is Invited: Small groups thrive when dialogue is encouraged. Leaders can create space for silence, recognizing that thoughtful reflection is not failure but a gift. Open-ended questions invite members to wrestle with Scripture and apply it personally. Conversation should also extend beyond the group gathering. Encouraging participation through midweek texts, shared meals, and service projects builds a rhythm of community. This ongoing engagement makes the small group more than a weekly event; it becomes a way of life together.

3. Context is Considered: The physical and relational setting of a group matters. The arrangement of space shapes whether members feel like contributors or spectators. Circles promote conversation, while rows unintentionally create an audience. Leaders should ensure there are enough seats available without making people feel restricted to "assigned spots." Even the atmosphere—lighting, seating comfort, and snacks—affects whether people feel welcomed and at ease. A thoughtful context communicates hospitality and creates the right environment for spiritual growth.

4. Confidentiality is Protected: For real transformation to happen, trust must be present. Groups need a clear commitment to privacy: what is shared in the group stays in the group. Proverbs 11:13 reminds us, *"Whoever goes about slandering reveals secrets, but he who is trustworthy in spirit keeps a thing covered."* Protecting confidentiality builds a safe space where honesty can flourish. When members are assured that their struggles will not leave the room, they are freed to share openly, and the group becomes a place of healing and grace.

5. Consistency is Practiced: A reliable rhythm helps members stay engaged and invested. Groups that meet on a predictable schedule with a steady flow and format create a sense of stability. This consistency demonstrates reliability and communicates that the group is a priority. In contrast, groups that meet sporadically often struggle to gain momentum or build trust. Commitment to regular gatherings shows that spiritual growth together is worth the investment of time and effort, reinforcing the value of shared discipleship.

6. Care through Hospitality is Offered: Hospitality reflects the heart of Christ and makes the group a place of belonging. The early church modeled this beautifully: *"They received their food with glad and generous hearts"* (Acts 2:46). Simple acts like offering snacks, greeting warmly at the door, or providing a comfortable meeting space create a sense of welcome. Hospitality is not about impressing others but about fostering belonging and embodying the love of Christ. When members feel cared for in practical ways, it softens hearts and opens them to deeper fellowship and discipleship.

Atmosphere is not a side issue—it communicates theology. A room arranged for participation declares that every believer has something to contribute (1 Peter 2:9). A group marked by courtesy, conversation, context, confidentiality, consistency, and care declares that the gospel creates a family where truth and love are lived out.[68]

---

[68] See Donahue, *Leading Life-Changing Small Groups*, 57–82; Gladen, *Small Groups with Purpose*, 115–36; Stanley, Willits, and Zempel, *Creating Community*, 121–43; Bowman and Donahue, *Coaching Life-Changing Small Group Leaders*, 98–112; Joy and Shelton, *The People of God*, 85–104; Guindon, *Disciple-Making Culture*, 167–88; Smith, "Essentials for Effective Small Group Facilitation," 221–35.

Dependence on the Spirit

No matter how well a leader prepares, the Spirit of God must empower the presentation. Jesus promised, *"The Helper, the Holy Spirit, whom the Father will send in my name, he will teach you all things and bring to your remembrance all that I have said to you"* (John 14:26).

Holy Spirit dependence is essential for every small group leader because it reminds us that transformation is ultimately the work of God, not human effort. Leaders can plan lessons, structure questions, and guide discussions, but without reliance on the Holy Spirit, their work risks becoming little more than human wisdom. Spirit dependence can be expressed in three key truths: prayerful preparation, prompted perception, and power in proclamation.

Prayerful preparation begins before the group ever meets. A leader who seeks God's guidance in advance acknowledges their need for His wisdom and illumination. Jesus promised that the Holy Spirit would teach and remind us of truth (John 14:26), and leaders must lean into that promise. By asking God to open their minds and hearts to the text before they guide others, leaders prepare not only their notes but also their souls.

Prompted perception means staying sensitive to the Spirit's leading in the moment. Discussions do not always unfold as expected, and sometimes the Spirit nudges a leader to pause, redirect, or emphasize a truth that was not originally in the plan. This requires humility and attentiveness, as seen in Paul's missionary journey when the Spirit redirected him away from Asia and toward Macedonia (Acts 16:6–10). A Spirit-dependent leader trusts God enough to adjust when He leads.

Power in proclamation is the recognition that fruit comes not from eloquence or clever teaching but from God's presence. The early disciples were noted as *"uneducated, common men,"* yet their boldness revealed that they had been with Jesus (Acts 4:13). In the same way, leaders can speak with confidence—not in themselves, but in God's Spirit, who empowers the Word to convict, encourage, and transform lives. Spirit dependence ensures that what happens in the small group is not merely instruction but encounter.

Before beginning small group, pause and pray silently for God's Spirit to guide your words, your tone, and the responses of those in the group.[69]

Teaching with Accountability

Presentation is not just about transmitting information—it is about transformation. That requires accountability. Elmer Towns reminds us, "Man must be doers of the Word, not hearers only."[70]

Accountability in presentation is vital for healthy small group leadership because it ensures that teaching is not just information but transformation. When leaders embrace accountability, they help members grow in both character and conduct, guiding them toward Christlikeness. This

---

[69] See Donahue, *Leading Life-Changing Small Groups*, 57–82; Gladen, *Small Groups with Purpose*, 115–36; Stanley, Willits, and Zempel, *Creating Community*, 121–43; Bowman and Donahue, *Coaching Life-Changing Small Group Leaders*, 98–112; Joy and Shelton, *The People of God*, 85–104; Guindon, *Disciple-Making Culture*, 167–88; Smith, "Essentials for Effective Small Group Facilitation," 221–35.

[70] Elmer Towns, How to Build a Successful Sunday School (Nashville: Thomas Nelson, 1982), 116.

accountability expresses itself in three interconnected ways: relational, scriptural, and instructional.

Relational accountability involves knowing the people in your group well enough to speak truth personally and lovingly. Like Nathan confronting David in 2 Samuel 12:1–7, accountability sometimes requires courage to challenge sin, but it also includes encouragement to press on in faith. True relationships allow space for both, reminding people that they are cared for too much to be left in complacency.

Scriptural accountability centers on the Word of God as the ultimate authority. Leaders are not accountable merely to their own opinions but to the truth of Scripture. As Romans 12:2 teaches, the renewing of the mind comes from God's Word, which confronts sin and points to transformation. When a leader consistently brings the group back to Scripture, accountability is rooted in God's standard rather than human judgment.

Instructional accountability highlights the weight of teaching. Proverbs 10:17 reminds us that rejecting correction hinders growth and misleads others. In the context of a small group, this means helping members see that obedience to God's Word is not optional. A leader's role is to clarify truth, warn against disobedience, and remind members that following Christ faithfully not only shapes their own walk but also influences those who look to them for example.

Biblical accountability is never harsh or detached; it is delivered in love. Keith Rose notes that in Scripture, accountability is always relational and personal, never merely institutional.[71]

Handling Difficult Moments

Even the most prayerful preparation cannot predict everything that will unfold in a group. Chapter 4 reminded us that wise leaders prepare for potential challenges. But during presentation, unexpected moments still come. These moments are not disruptions to dread, they are opportunities to shepherd people with grace and truth.[72] This subject is also explored more in Chapter 13.

- **When discussion drifts:** Affirm the contribution, then guide the group back to the passage: "That's a helpful thought. Let's connect it to what this verse is saying."

- **When someone dominates:** Honor their input while opening space for others: "Thank you for sharing. I'd love to hear what others think as well."

- **When silence lingers:** Don't panic. Silence often means people are reflecting. You can rephrase the question or share briefly from your own walk to restart dialogue.

---

[71] Keith Rose, "Accountability in the Bible: Relational and Redemptive," Bible.org, accessed August 23, 2025, https://bible.org/article/accountability-bible-relational-and-redemptive.

[72] See Donahue, *Leading Life-Changing Small Groups*, 57–82; Gladen, *Small Groups with Purpose*, 115–36; Stanley, Willits, and Zempel, *Creating Community*, 121–43; Bowman and Donahue, *Coaching Life-Changing Small Group Leaders*, 98–112; Joy and Shelton, *The People of God*, 85–104; Guindon, *Disciple-Making Culture*, 167–88; Smith, "Essentials for Effective Small Group Facilitation," 221–35.

- **When sensitive issues arise:** Anchor the group in Scripture rather than opinions. A simple phrase like, "Let's see how God's Word speaks to this," helps keep the focus on truth.

Such moments stretch leaders in real time. More than polished answers, what people notice is your tone, your patience, and your reliance on God's Word. The way you respond in difficulty may communicate the gospel as powerfully as the lesson itself.[73]

Facilitating Discussion vs. Lecturing

The temptation for leaders is to lecture. Lecturing feels efficient, safe, and controlled. But small groups thrive when members wrestle with Scripture together. Discussion deepens ownership. Jesus often taught by asking questions that drew people into truth (Matthew 16:15). Similarly, leaders shepherd best by inviting dialogue.[74] Ken Braddy emphasizes that "the

---

[73] See Donahue, *Leading Life-Changing Small Groups*, 57–82; Gladen, *Small Groups with Purpose*, 115–36; Stanley, Willits, and Zempel, *Creating Community*, 121–43; Bowman and Donahue, *Coaching Life-Changing Small Group Leaders*, 98–112; Joy and Shelton, *The People of God*, 85–104; Guindon, *Disciple-Making Culture*, 167–88; Smith, "Essentials for Effective Small Group Facilitation," 221–35.

[74] See Craig J. Blomberg and Jennifer Foutz Markley, *The Cradle, the Cross, and the Crown: An Introduction to the New Testament* (2nd ed.; Nashville: B&H Academic, 2016), 48–52; Andy Stanley and Bill Willits, *Creating Community: Five Keys to Building a Small Group Culture* (Colorado Springs: Multnomah, 2004), 95–112; Steve Gladen, *Leading Small Groups with Purpose: Everything You Need to Lead a Healthy Group* (Grand Rapids: Baker Books, 2012), 141–65; Bill Donahue, *Building a Church of Small Groups: A Place Where Nobody Stands Alone* (Grand Rapids: Zondervan, 2001), 133–49; Jim Putman and Bobby Harrington, *DiscipleShift: Five Steps That Help Your Church to Make Disciples Who Make Disciples* (Grand Rapids: Zondervan, 2013), 183–202.

higher the level of engagement, the more likely people are to remember and apply what they learn."[75]

Effective discussion strategies help small groups move from passive listening to active engagement. These strategies give every member an opportunity to contribute, reflect, and process what God is teaching them. One method is the use of **buzz groups**, where members break into pairs or trios to discuss a question in a smaller, safer setting before sharing with the larger group. Similarly, a **pair and share** allows two individuals to process a scenario together, giving them space to think deeply and build confidence before contributing to the wider discussion.

Another strategy is the **circular response**, in which each person around the circle offers a brief answer to the same question. This ensures that every voice is heard and guards against a few individuals dominating the conversation. Likewise, **sentence completion** prompts such as, "One way I've seen God's faithfulness this week is…" provide simple yet powerful opportunities for personal reflection and testimony. These techniques invite participation and allow group members to connect Scripture with their daily lives in practical ways.

The leader's role in these strategies is not to impress the group with theological knowledge or lengthy explanations but to shepherd the discussion back to God's Word. True transformation happens not when people are awed by a leader's insight but when they encounter God's truth together and are challenged to live it out. A wise leader uses these methods to create dialogue, foster reflection, and keep the focus centered

[75] Ken Braddy, Breathing Life into Sunday School (Nashville: B&H Publishing, 2015), 84

on Scripture, ensuring that the group grows in both understanding and obedience.[76]

Asking Good Questions

Questions are the backbone of meaningful group discussion. They invite participation, spark reflection, and lead people beyond passive listening to active discovery. Jesus Himself modeled the power of questions when He asked His disciples, *"Who do you say that I am?"* (Matthew 16:15). That single question did more than test knowledge; it drew His followers into a deeper understanding of His identity and demanded a personal response. In the same way, wise small group leaders use questions to guide their members into truth, conviction, and transformation.

Effective small group questions come in several forms. **Open-ended questions** avoid simple yes-or-no answers and instead encourage reflection. For example, asking "What does this verse reveal about God's character?" prompts deeper thought than "Do you believe this verse?" **Scripture-centered questions** are equally important because they keep the group anchored in God's Word rather than drifting into speculation or personal opinion. **Application-oriented questions** help members take the step from knowledge to obedience. It is not enough to merely understand the text; the goal is to live it out together.

---

[76] See Donahue, *Leading Life-Changing Small Groups*, 57–82; Gladen, *Small Groups with Purpose*, 115–36; Stanley, Willits, and Zempel, *Creating Community*, 121–43; Bowman and Donahue, *Coaching Life-Changing Small Group Leaders*, 98–112; Joy and Shelton, *The People of God*, 85–104; Guindon, *Disciple-Making Culture*, 167–88; Smith, "Essentials for Effective Small Group Facilitation," 221–35.

A helpful framework for application-oriented discussion is **Head, Heart, Hands**. This simple pattern keeps the focus practical and holistic. The **Head** asks, "What does this passage say?"—clarifying the truth of the text. The **Heart** asks, "How does this truth convict or comfort me?"—personalizing the message. Finally, the **Hands** ask, "What should I do differently this week?"—moving from reflection to action. When groups follow this framework, the discussion naturally progresses from comprehension, to conviction, to concrete steps of obedience.[77]

Using Illustrations and Stories

Jesus taught profound truths through stories, parables, and examples drawn from everyday life. A mustard seed, a lamp, a vineyard, all were simple illustrations that carried eternal weight. Stories connect the head and heart, moving truth from theory into reality.[78]

Effective illustrations in group presentation should be:

- **Concise:** Keep the illustrations short so the story supports the Scripture rather than overshadowing it.

- **Connected:** Tie the stories directly to the passage or principle being discussed.

---

[77] See Blomberg and Markley, *Cradle, the Cross, and the Crown*, 48–52; Stanley and Willits, *Creating Community*, 95–112; Gladen, *Leading Small Groups with Purpose*, 141–65; Donahue, *Building a Church of Small Groups*, 133–49; Putman and Harrington, *DiscipleShift*, 183–202.

[78] See Blomberg and Markley, *Cradle, the Cross, and the Crown*, 48–52; Stanley and Willits, *Creating Community*, 95–112; Gladen, *Leading Small Groups with Purpose*, 141–65; Donahue, *Building a Church of Small Groups*, 133–49; Putman and Harrington, *DiscipleShift*, 183–202.

- **Christ-Centered:** Use the illustrations to highlight God's character, Christ's work, and the call to obedience, not just human interest.

Leaders can draw from personal testimony, group experiences, or biblical narratives. For example: when teaching on God's provision, share a story of answered prayer in your own life. Stories help people remember the truth long after the group ends.[79]

Presenting with Heart, Not Just Head

Presentation must go beyond intellectual clarity. Truth should be taught with warmth, conviction, and authenticity. John Maxwell notes that "people buy into the leader before they buy into the vision."[80] Authenticity builds trust, and trust earns the right to lead.

That means the following for small group leaders:

- Sharing personally when appropriate.
- Speaking with conviction, not mere recitation.
- Demonstrating humility, acknowledging when you don't have all the answers.

---

[79] See Blomberg and Markley, *Cradle, the Cross, and the Crown*, 48–52; Stanley and Willits, *Creating Community*, 95–112; Gladen, *Leading Small Groups with Purpose*, 141–65; Donahue, *Building a Church of Small Groups*, 133–49; Putman and Harrington, *DiscipleShift*, 183–202.

[80] John C. Maxwell, The 21 Irrefutable Laws of Leadership (Nashville: Thomas Nelson, 2007), 43.

Group members often remember the spirit of your presentation more than the specifics. They will recall whether you were passionate, approachable, and Holy Spirit-led.[81]

Practical Helps for Presentation

Effective presentation in a small group is not about perfect polish or impressive delivery. Instead, it is about intentional habits that keep people engaged with God's Word and foster genuine growth. A leader's goal is not to perform but to shepherd, creating an environment where truth is heard, hearts are engaged, and lives are transformed. Several practical helps can guide leaders in presenting with clarity and care.

One important practice is to **craft questions** in advance. Preparing three to five open-ended questions that connect directly to the text ensures the discussion stays focused and invites reflection. Alongside this, leaders must **control the conversation** by striking a balance between talking and listening. A healthy rhythm is for the leader to guide about one-third of the time and allow the group to engage about two-thirds. This shift keeps participation high and prevents the group from becoming a lecture.

Leaders should also **center on Scripture** by having members read passages aloud together. This reinforces that

---

[81] See Bill Donahue, *Leading Life-Changing Small Groups* (3rd ed.; Grand Rapids: Zondervan, 2012), 57–78; Steve Gladen, *Leading Small Groups with Purpose: Everything You Need to Lead a Healthy Group* (Grand Rapids: Baker Books, 2012), 133–62; Andy Stanley and Bill Willits, *Creating Community: Five Keys to Building a Small Group Culture* (Colorado Springs: Multnomah, 2004), 87–104; John C. Maxwell, *The 21 Irrefutable Laws of Leadership* (10th Anniversary ed.; Nashville: Thomas Nelson, 2007), 151–69; Jim Putman and Bobby Harrington, *DiscipleShift: Five Steps That Help Your Church to Make Disciples Who Make Disciples* (Grand Rapids: Zondervan, 2013), 183–202.

God's Word, not the leader's opinions, is the primary authority (2 Timothy 3:16–17). At the same time, leaders must be willing to **change with context**, adapting their style to the group's needs. Some weeks may call for more direct teaching, while others may benefit from open sharing or extended prayer, just as Paul shifted his direction in response to the Spirit's leading (Acts 16:6–10).

Presentation is also about presence. A leader's **countenance communicates** as much as their words, smiling, making eye contact, and avoiding the temptation to hide behind your notes helps create a welcoming atmosphere. **Clarity** matters as well: speaking with clear words, a varied tone, and a steady pace keeps members engaged and ensures the message is understood. Tools such as slides, videos, or visuals can enhance learning, but leaders should use them carefully so they support rather than overshadow Scripture.

Finally, leaders must look beyond themselves by **cultivating new leaders**. Handing off portions of the discussion to others not only lightens the leader's load but also trains future facilitators, ensuring the group has the potential to multiply. This practice models shared responsibility and encourages members to step into greater ownership of their discipleship journey.

When these practical helps are consistently applied, presentation becomes more than just managing a meeting. It transforms into a ministry of shepherding, where God's Word remains central, people are drawn into active participation, and discipleship takes root in ways that last.[82]

Conclusion: Presentation as Shepherding

At its heart, presentation is shepherding God's people through His Word. It is not about polished communication but about faithful facilitation. Nehemiah 8:8 models the goal, *"They read from the book, from the Law of God, clearly, and they gave the sense, so that the people understood the reading."*

Faithful presentation means:
- Depending on the Holy Spirit.
- Creating a safe and engaging atmosphere.
- Asking good questions that invite ownership.
- Guiding with accountability and humility.
- Sharing the Word with both clarity and warmth.

But let's pause and linger on this truth: many small group leaders feel the pressure to sound like polished preachers, seminary-trained teachers, or professional communicators. That burden is not from the Lord. He has not called you to perform but to shepherd. Your effectiveness is not measured by eloquence, but by obedience.

You are not defined by what you are not—you are defined by what God says you are. You are a child of God, entrusted with His Word and called to lead His people in community. Paul reminded the Corinthians, *"But we have this treasure in*

---

[82] See Donahue, *Leading Life-Changing Small Groups*, 57–78; Gladen, *Leading Small Groups with Purpose*, 133–62; Stanley and Willits, *Creating Community*, 87–104; Maxwell, 21 *Irrefutable Laws of Leadership*, 151–69; Putman and Harrington, *DiscipleShift*, 183–202.

jars of clay, to show that the surpassing power belongs to God and not to us" (2 Corinthians 4:7). Your weakness does not disqualify you; it displays His strength.

As you present, remember that people will recall not just what you taught but how you led—with love, authenticity, and Spirit-led conviction. Your role is not to impress but to point to Christ. Presentation is an act of shepherding: guiding God's people to encounter His living Word together. And in that faithful act, God is pleased, His people are fed, and Christ is exalted.

Reflection Questions

1. Does my group feel safe to ask honest questions and share struggles?

2. Do I invite response, or do I dominate the conversation?

3. Am I using Scripture as the central voice in the group?

4. Do I build accountability into our discussions, pointing people toward obedience?

Chapter 6: Participation

"From him the whole body, joined and held together by every supporting ligament, grows and builds itself up in love, as each part does its work." – Ephesians 4:16 (NIV)

A healthy small group is not a one-man show. It is the body of Christ functioning together. Every member has a role to play. Participation is both the means and the fruit of discipleship. When people engage, they move from being mere attenders to becoming active disciples who contribute to the health of the group and the mission of Christ.

Why Participation Matters

Participation distinguishes a class from a community. A small group that relies only on the leader quickly becomes stagnant. If the leader is absent, the group falters. But when every member participates, the group grows stronger, deeper, and wider.

Paul describes the church as a body, *"For the body does not consist of one member but of many...If one member suffers, all suffer together; if one member is honored, all rejoice together. Now you are the body of Christ and individually members of it"* (1 Corinthians 12:14, 26–27).

Participation is the difference between spectatorship and discipleship. When everyone contributes, members not only learn but live out the call of God together.[83]

Theology of Participation

Participation in the body of Christ is not simply practical but profoundly theological. From the very beginning, God designed His people to live in interdependence. The Triune God—Father, Son, and Spirit—exists in eternal fellowship and mutual glorification. Small group participation mirrors this divine fellowship, reminding us that isolation is contrary to God's nature and His design for His people (Genesis 2:18; John 17:21).

Peter describes the church as a *"royal priesthood"* (1 Peter 2:9), meaning that every believer is called into ministry, prayer, and proclamation—not just a select few. Paul echoes this in Romans 12, emphasizing that though *"we, though many, are one body in Christ, and individually members one of another"* (Romans 12:5), each has distinct gifts meant for the common good (Romans 12:6–8). Participation, then, is not an optional

---

[83] See Bill Donahue, *Building a Church of Small Groups: A Place Where Nobody Stands Alone* (Grand Rapids: Zondervan, 2001), 45–66; Steve Gladen, *Small Groups with Purpose: How to Create Healthy Communities* (Grand Rapids: Baker Books, 2011), 23–52; M. Scott Boren, Missional *Small Groups: Becoming a Community That Makes a Difference in the World* (Grand Rapids: Baker Books, 2010), 71–95; Andy Stanley and Bill Willits, *Creating Community: Five Keys to Building a Small Group Culture* (Colorado Springs: Multnomah, 2004), 29–54; Jim Egli and Dwight Marable, *Small Groups, Big Impact: Connecting People to God and One Another in Healthy Groups* (St. Charles, IL: ChurchSmart Resources, 2011), 17–34; Michael J. Anthony, "Small Groups in Protestant Churches: A Historical Overview," *Christian Education Journal* 3, no. 2 (2006): 257–72; Joel Comiskey, "The Value of Participating in Small Groups," *Journal of the American Society for Church Growth* 10 (1999): 31–46.

activity; it is a necessity for a disciple of Christ. To neglect participation is to deny the reality of the Holy Spirit's gifting (1 Corinthians 12; Romans 12:3-8) and the priesthood of believers.[84] Leaders, are we helping our small group members become more than spectators?

Every Member Engaged

Spectatorship is the enemy of discipleship. Paul reminds us in 1 Corinthians 12 that the Church is one body with many parts, each uniquely gifted and essential to the whole. *"The eye cannot say to the hand, 'I have no need of you,' nor again the head to the feet, 'I have no need of you'"* (1 Corinthians 12:21). A small group functions the same way: if only the leader speaks, the group becomes a lecture hall; but when every member participates, it becomes a family.

What does engagement look like? It means more than showing up, sitting down, and absorbing information. True engagement happens when people use their gifts, share their stories, and act on their calling together. Leaders must intentionally invite members into dialogue, responsibility, and ownership.

Rob Wegner and Brian Phipps describe this in their "GPS" model, Gifts, Passions, and Story. They argue that "every believer is divinely designed and spiritually empowered to contribute meaningfully to God's mission" and that by understanding how God has wired them, members can live

---

[84] See Donahue, *Building a Church of Small Groups*, 45–66; Gladen, *Small Groups with Purpose*, 23–52; Boren, *Missional Small Groups*, 71–95; Stanley and Willits, Creating Community, 29–54; Egli and Marable, *Small Groups, Big Impact*, 17–34; Anthony, "Small Groups in Protestant Churches," 257–72; Comiskey, "Value of Participating in Small Groups," 31–46.

with clarity and intentionality in both church and community.[85] Discovering one's spiritual gifts is not an academic exercise; it is the pathway to meaningful service.

Unfortunately, many groups unintentionally encourage passivity, members are welcomed to sit quietly, listen, and leave. That may produce attenders, but it does not form disciples. Leaders must help people move from the seat to the street, living out their discipleship beyond the meeting. When members discover their God-given gifts, passions, and experiences, they become equipped not just to consume but to contribute.

This kind of engagement requires time, prayer, and shared responsibility. A leader cannot do it alone. Other group members, church leaders, and pastors should be invited into the process of equipping people to serve. By identifying gifts and encouraging participation, small groups can help believers step fully into the calling God has placed on their lives. Participation in a small group is not optional; it is vital. We are not called to be spectators; we are called to be disciples who make disciples.[86]

[85] Rob Wegner and Brian Phipps, Find Your Place: Locating Your Calling Through Your Gifts, Passions, and Story (Grand Rapids: Zondervan, 2019), 25–27.

[86] See Donahue, *Building a Church of Small Groups*, 45–66; Gladen, *Small Groups with Purpose*, 23–52; Boren, *Missional Small Groups*, 71–95; Stanley and Willits, Creating Community, 29–54; Egli and Marable, *Small Groups, Big Impact*, 17–34; Anthony, "Small Groups in Protestant Churches," 257–72; Comiskey, "Value of Participating in Small Groups," 31–46.

Barriers to Participation

While God calls all believers to contribute, real obstacles often hinder participation. Some remain silent out of fear of judgment, lack of biblical confidence, or past wounds from unhealthy group experiences. Others dominate conversation because of insecurity or the need for control.

Scripture calls leaders to shepherd both types with patience and gentleness: *"Brothers, if anyone is caught in any transgression, you who are spiritual should restore him in a spirit of gentleness"* (Galatians 6:1). Leaders are to create a safe space where authenticity is valued and participation flows from grace rather than pressure.

Bill Donahue observes that participation thrives when groups emphasize authenticity over performance, noting that transformation comes not through polished answers but through honest engagement.[87] Larry Osborne adds that groups stagnate when they allow cliques or unchecked monopolization of discussion.[88] Recognizing these barriers and addressing them with love protects the integrity of participation.

Participation in Prayer

One of the most powerful ways members can engage in a small group is through prayer. Prayer is not simply a closing ritual or a filler between discussion questions; it is a vital expression of dependence on God and an acknowledgment that the Spirit is the one who brings transformation. This subject is

---

[87] Bill Donahue, Leading Life-Changing Small Groups, 2nd ed. (Grand Rapids: Zondervan, 2012).

[88] Larry Osborne, Sticky Church (Grand Rapids: Zondervan, 2008).

explored in greater detail in Chapter 7, but Acts 4:23–31 gives us a vivid picture of its impact. When the early believers lifted their voices together in prayer, the result was a renewed boldness and empowerment by the Holy Spirit. In the same way, prayer participation in small groups reinforces the truth that these gatherings are not merely Bible classes but worshiping communities where God's presence is sought and experienced.

Leaders play a key role in fostering this kind of prayerful culture. They can rotate prayer leadership each week, giving different members the opportunity to guide the group in conversation with God. They can encourage members to pray Scripture over one another, such as using Psalm 23 as a framework to intercede for comfort, guidance, and provision. They can also create space for more intimate prayer by breaking the group into smaller pairs or triads, where individuals may feel freer to share specific requests and pray more personally. These practices not only deepen participation but also cultivate a shared sense of responsibility and spiritual growth within the group.

Dietrich Bonhoeffer emphasized that Christian community is sustained through shared intercession, writing that "a Christian fellowship lives and exists by the intercession of its members for one another, or it collapses."[89] When every member prays, the group moves from passivity to active

---

[89] Dietrich Bonhoeffer, Life Together, trans. John W. Doberstein (San Francisco: Harper & Row, 1954), 86.

spiritual warfare, reinforcing dependence on God rather than human effort.[90]

Tool for Engaging Every Member

Small group leaders often wrestle with the question, "How do I get people more engaged?" While the answer is not complicated, but it does require intentionality. Engagement flows out of a clear discipleship rhythm—Discover, Deploy, and Disciple—that helps people not only participate but also grow as followers of Jesus. When this rhythm is embraced, groups move beyond being gatherings of passive listeners and become communities where every member actively contributes to the mission of Christ.

The first step is **Discover**. Leaders can help members identify their God-given gifts, passions, and experiences. As 1 Corinthians 12 reminds us, every believer has a role to play in the body of Christ, and no contribution is insignificant. Practical tools, like Find Your Place and its GPS framework— Gifts, Passions, and Story—provide a structured way for people to see how God has uniquely shaped them.[91] Discovery can happen during group discussions, in one-on-one conversations, or even through assignments outside the group. A helpful resource for this process is the free GPS Assessment from Disciples Made, available at www.disciplesmade.com/

---

[90] See Donahue, *Building a Church of Small Groups*, 45–66; Gladen, *Small Groups with Purpose*, 23–52; Boren, *Missional Small Groups*, 71–95; Stanley and Willits, Creating Community, 29–54; Egli and Marable, *Small Groups, Big Impact*, 17–34; Anthony, "Small Groups in Protestant Churches," 257–72; Comiskey, "Value of Participating in Small Groups," 31–46.

[91] Wegner and Phipps, Find Your Place, 25–27.

find-your-place. By guiding people through discovery, leaders affirm that every person has a place in God's plan.

The second step is **Deploy**. Once gifts are uncovered, leaders should help members put them into practice. This could mean inviting someone to lead prayer, host a gathering, organize a fellowship event, or spearhead a service project. As Paul wrote, *"To each is given the manifestation of the Spirit for the common good"* (1 Corinthians 12:7). Deployment shifts engagement from theory to action, giving disciples a sense of ownership and responsibility within the group.[92]

Finally, the third step is **Disciple**. Engagement is never just about filling roles or completing tasks; it is about transformation. Leaders are called to walk alongside members, offering encouragement, giving feedback, and consistently pointing them back to Christ. True discipleship is about multiplication—raising up new leaders, training apprentices, and equipping disciple-makers who will carry the mission forward. As Paul instructed Timothy, "What you have heard from me in the presence of many witnesses entrust to faithful men, who will be able to teach others also" (2 Timothy 2:2). In this way, discipleship engagement extends far beyond the group itself, fueling the growth and impact of the kingdom.[93]

---

[92] See Donahue, *Building a Church of Small Groups*, 45–66; Gladen, *Small Groups with Purpose*, 23–52; Boren, *Missional Small Groups*, 71–95; Stanley and Willits, Creating Community, 29–54; Egli and Marable, *Small Groups, Big Impact*, 17–34; Anthony, "Small Groups in Protestant Churches," 257–72; Comiskey, "Value of Participating in Small Groups," 31–46.

[93] See Donahue, *Building a Church of Small Groups*, 45–66; Gladen, *Small Groups with Purpose*, 23–52; Boren, *Missional Small Groups*, 71–95; Stanley and Willits, Creating Community, 29–54; Egli and Marable, *Small Groups, Big Impact*, 17–34; Anthony, "Small Groups in Protestant Churches," 257–72; Comiskey, "Value of Participating in Small Groups," 31–46.

Putting It Into Practice

A healthy small group must be intentional about creating spaces for every member to grow and participate. One way to do this is to set aside a dedicated night for **Discover**, allowing group members to share their passions, stories, and strengths so that relationships deepen and hidden gifts emerge. Beyond discovery, the group should also prioritize **Deploy**, assigning weekly opportunities for members to serve and rotating roles so that everyone has the chance to contribute meaningfully. Finally, lasting transformation comes through **Disciple rhythms**, where leaders consistently check in with members, pray over them, and encourage them to step into leadership beyond the group. This can be guided by the 4M Rhythm, **Meet, Model, Mentor, and Multiply,** which ensures that discipleship flows outward in both intentionality and practice. Together, these rhythms help a small group move from simply meeting to truly multiplying disciples.[94]

The **4 M Rhythm** provides small group leaders with a simple yet powerful framework for intentional disciple-making. Each step builds on the other, creating a pathway that moves people from initial connection to full multiplication in the mission of Christ. When practiced consistently, this rhythm ensures that discipleship is not left to chance but becomes a deliberate, relational process that mirrors the way Jesus Himself invested in His followers.

---

[94] See Donahue, *Building a Church of Small Groups*, 45–66; Gladen, *Small Groups with Purpose*, 23–52; Boren, *Missional Small Groups*, 71–95; Stanley and Willits, Creating Community, 29–54; Egli and Marable, *Small Groups, Big Impact*, 17–34; Anthony, "Small Groups in Protestant Churches," 257–72; Comiskey, "Value of Participating in Small Groups," 31–46.

The first step is **Meet**. Just as Jesus appointed the twelve *"so that they might be with him"* (Mark 3:14), leaders are called to build consistency in relationships. Meeting regularly communicates commitment, fosters trust, and provides the relational context where spiritual growth can take root. Without consistency, discipleship remains shallow; with it, relationships deepen and lives are transformed.

The second step is **Model**. Paul encouraged the Corinthians, *"Be imitators of me, as I am of Christ"* (1 Corinthians 11:1). Discipleship is not simply about transferring information but about demonstrating a Christ-centered life. Leaders model faithfulness in prayer, obedience to Scripture, love in relationships, and integrity in daily life. By showing what it looks like to follow Jesus, they give others a living example to follow.

The third step is **Mentor**. This involves walking alongside others with intentional coaching, encouragement, and prayer. As Paul exhorted Timothy, leaders are to invest personally, offering feedback and guiding others to maturity in their walk with Christ (2 Timothy 2:2a). Mentoring provides space for questions, accountability, and personal encouragement, helping disciples grow stronger and more confident in their faith.

The final step is **Multiply**. True discipleship is not complete until it reproduces. Paul's full vision for Timothy was that he would entrust what he learned *"to faithful men, who will be able to teach others also"* (2 Timothy 2:2b). Leaders must release and empower others to lead, equipping them to start new groups and continue the cycle of disciple-making. Multiplication ensures that the mission of Christ does not stop with one group but spreads outward, creating a ripple effect of transformed lives.

The *Discover → Deploy → Disciple Tool* is a simple yet powerful framework that shifts participation from being an afterthought to becoming the very heartbeat of your group's discipleship pathway. Rather than leaving engagement to chance, this tool provides intentional steps that help every member identify their gifts, put them into practice, and grow as multiplying disciples of Jesus. To guide this process, use the *Small Group Participation Pathway Chart,* see the following page. The chart is a clear overview of the rhythm, the *Participation Tracker* to monitor members' progress and next steps, and the *Individual Plan* for one-on-one coaching and personalized growth (see Appendices 2 and 3). By combining these tools, leaders can create a culture where participation is not optional but expected, where discipleship is not theoretical but practical, and where every believer is equipped to discover, deploy, and disciple for the sake of Christ's mission.[95]

[95] See Donahue, *Building a Church of Small Groups*, 45–66; Gladen, *Small Groups with Purpose*, 23–52; Boren, *Missional Small Groups*, 71–95; Stanley and Willits, Creating Community, 29–54; Egli and Marable, *Small Groups, Big Impact*, 17–34; Anthony, "Small Groups in Protestant Churches," 257–72; Comiskey, "Value of Participating in Small Groups," 31–46.

Small Group Participation Pathway
Discover → Deploy → Disciple

DISCOVER

Scripture: 1 Cor. 12; Rom. 12:6-8

Ask: What gifts, passions, abilities and experiences?

Tool:. find a credible spiritual gift test.

↓

DEPLOY

Scripture: 1 Cor. 12:7; Eph. 4:12

Ask: What small role will you try this month?

Roles: Prayer leader, Host, Greeter, Scripture reader, Service project lead.

↓

DISCIPLE

Scripture: 2 Tim. 2:2; Matt. 28:19 20

Ask: Who are you investing in? Who could you apprentice?

Rhythm (4M): Meet • Model • Mentor • Multiply

Drawing Out the Quiet, Guiding the Talkative

Not every member engages in the same way. Some remain quiet out of fear, shyness, or uncertainty about their knowledge of Scripture. Others dominate conversation, often out of enthusiasm or the desire to process thoughts verbally. Both tendencies are common in groups and must be shepherded with grace and intentionality.[96]

Calling on the Quiet Gently

Quiet members often need permission to share. Here are a few strategies I have used in leading small groups when dealing with silent or quiet members. Leaders can take several intentional steps to engage their group more effectively, such as:

- **Use names carefully:** "Sarah, what do you think about this passage?" A gentle invitation communicates value without pressure.

- **Affirm contributions:** Even short answers can be reinforced: "That's a great point; thank you for sharing." This builds confidence for future participation.

- **Provide space for silence:** Don't rush to fill every pause. Silence allows quieter voices the chance to enter.

---

[96] See Donahue, *Building a Church of Small Groups*, 45–66; Gladen, *Small Groups with Purpose*, 23–52; Boren, *Missional Small Groups*, 71–95; Stanley and Willits, Creating Community, 29–54; Egli and Marable, *Small Groups, Big Impact*, 17–34; Anthony, "Small Groups in Protestant Churches," 257–72; Comiskey, "Value of Participating in Small Groups," 31–46.

- **Offer smaller settings:** Pair or triad discussions before sharing with the larger group can help hesitant members speak more freely.

Proverbs reminds us that *"the purposes in a man's heart is like deep water, but a man of understanding will draw it out"* (Proverbs 20:5). The wise leader patiently draws out what God has placed in others.[97]

Channeling the Talkative Wisely

Talkative members often bring energy and passion, but without guidance they can unintentionally discourage others from speaking. When a few individuals begin to dominate discussion, leaders can guide the group toward balance by taking the following approaches:

- **Thank them first:** Acknowledge their contribution so they feel heard.

- **Summarize their point:** Capture their main idea briefly, then transition: "That's helpful. Let's hear how others see this."

- **Redirect with purpose:** Invite balance: "I'd love to hear from someone who hasn't spoken yet."

---

[97] See Donahue, *Building a Church of Small Groups*, 45–66; Gladen, *Small Groups with Purpose*, 23–52; Boren, *Missional Small Groups*, 71–95; Stanley and Willits, Creating Community, 29–54; Egli and Marable, *Small Groups, Big Impact*, 17–34; Anthony, "Small Groups in Protestant Churches," 257–72; Comiskey, "Value of Participating in Small Groups," 31–46.

- **Set gentle boundaries:** If one person consistently monopolizes, address it privately with affirmation and encouragement toward self-awareness.

Paul's words in Philippians 2:3–4 remind us that participation is not about self-promotion but about humility, *"in humility count others more significant than yourselves. Let each of you look not only to his own interests, but also to the interests of others."*[98]

The Goal: Shared Engagement

The aim is not equal airtime but healthy engagement where all voices are valued. A small group flourishes when diversity of perspectives is heard and the body of Christ functions together. As 1 Corinthians 14:26 reminds us, *"When you come together, each one has a hymn, a lesson, a revelation, a tongue, or an interpretation. Let all things be done for building up."*

Drawing out the quiet and guiding the talkative are not mechanical techniques but shepherding practices that cultivate mutual respect, authentic fellowship, and discipleship growth.

Creating Opportunities for Participation

Participation must be nurtured with intentionality rather than left to chance. In order for every member to grow and contribute, opportunities must be created where involvement is

---

[98] See Donahue, *Building a Church of Small Groups*, 45–66; Gladen, *Small Groups with Purpose*, 23–52; Boren, *Missional Small Groups*, 71–95; Stanley and Willits, Creating Community, 29–54; Egli and Marable, *Small Groups, Big Impact*, 17–34; Anthony, "Small Groups in Protestant Churches," 257–72; Comiskey, "Value of Participating in Small Groups," 31–46.

both expected and encouraged. This participation can be cultivated in three key areas.

In the Lesson

- Use open-ended questions to invite dialogue.
- Encourage members to read Scripture aloud.
- Allow different voices to share testimonies, insights, or struggles.

In Life Together

- Challenge members to connect outside of weekly meetings through meals, texts, and prayer partners.
- Foster accountability by pairing members for spiritual check-ins (Proverbs 27:17).

In Leadership

- Involve others in facilitating prayer, welcoming, or organizing service projects.
- Rotate responsibilities so ownership is shared.

Participation is not about everyone doing the same thing, but about everyone doing something. True engagement happens when each person contributes according to their gifts and abilities (1 Corinthians 12:7). How can you better cultivate participation in your small group?[99]

---

[99] See Donahue, *Building a Church of Small Groups*, 45–66; Gladen, *Small Groups with Purpose*, 23–52; Boren, *Missional Small Groups*, 71–95; Stanley and Willits, Creating Community, 29–54; Egli and Marable, *Small Groups, Big Impact*, 17–34; Anthony, "Small Groups in Protestant Churches," 257–72; Comiskey, "Value of Participating in Small Groups," 31–46.

Encouraging Ownership Through Shared Roles

When members serve, they move from consumers to contributors. Leaders can delegate roles in their small group such as:

- Hosting the meeting.
- Leading prayer.
- Sharing a testimony.
- Organizing service projects.

Ken Braddy emphasizes that leaders should "stop recruiting teachers and start developing leaders," noting that many more are ready to lead than we often realize.[100]

Developing Apprentice Leaders

The ultimate form of participation is leadership multiplication. David Francis stresses that an apprentice teacher is the number one sign that a group is serious about reaching others for Christ.[101] Apprenticeship is not substitution, it is equipping.[102]

A leadership pipeline provides a clear and intentional pathway for developing future leaders, ensuring that discipleship is always moving forward. This simple apprentice model offers four stages that make the process both practical

---

[100] Ken Braddy, Breathing Life into Sunday School (Nashville: LifeWay Press, 2019), 45.

[101] Davide Francis, Missionary Sunday School (Nashville: LifeWay Press, 2011), 37.

[102] Braddy, *Breathing Life into Sunday School*, 45.

and reproducible. First, in the **Observe** stage, the apprentice simply watches the leader, gaining a vision for what faithful leadership looks like in action. Second, in the **Assist** stage, the apprentice begins helping in small, manageable ways, learning through participation while still under guidance. Third, in the **Lead** stage, the apprentice steps into responsibility, taking the lead while the leader provides encouragement, feedback, and support. Finally, in the **Send** stage, the apprentice is equipped and released to launch a new group, beginning the cycle again with their own apprentice. This simple pipeline—explained more fully in chapter 11—gives a refined understanding of how to move people from watching to leading, multiplying leadership in a sustainable, biblical way. It not only ensures that no one leads alone but also that the church continually raises up new shepherds to care for God's people.

Re-Engaging Absent Members

If you have been a small group leader for more than a few months, you know the challenge of inactive members. People who once attended regularly sometimes drift away. The question is: how do we re-engage them?

Over the years I've learned that this requires both intentionality and the participation of the whole group. Paul reminds us in 1 Corinthians 12 that we are one body with many parts. Some members have the gift of hospitality, others of relational connection—use those gifts to help bring people back. Re-engagement is not the sole responsibility of the leader; it is the work of the group as an unit. When I have asked people why they stopped attending a small group, the most common answers I hear are:

- "It felt like a clique."

- "I didn't feel welcome."

- "I didn't know anyone, and everyone else already knew each other."

- "I felt like an outsider."

Notice what is missing in these statements. Very few people say they left because they disliked the teacher or the Bible study. More often, their absence has to do with how the group participates in welcoming, greeting, and including others. Sometimes these reasons may sound like excuses, but often they reflect very real feelings. As leaders, we cannot simply dismiss them.[103]

Shepherding means addressing barriers to belonging and doing everything possible to help people feel engaged in discipleship. Here are some practical steps to pursue those who have drifted out of the group:

- **Contact Them:** Reach out with a call, text, or handwritten note. Simple communication goes a long way.

- **Connect Personally:** Share a meal, coffee, or one-on-one conversation. Often people return when they feel personally noticed and valued.

- **Create On-Ramps:** Fellowship events or informal gatherings provide easier re-entry than a formal Bible study session.

---

[103] Braddy, Breathing Life into Sunday School, 45-47.

- **Cover Them in Prayer:** Intercede regularly for inactive members. Prayer softens hearts and opens doors for reconnection.

Re-engagement is shepherding. We can choose to ignore inactive members and blame them for leaving, or we can do everything within our power to make them feel valued, included, and discipled. A culture of participation means no one is left behind.

Participation Beyond the Group

Healthy groups don't just meet, they serve. Jesus said, *"Let your light shine before others, so that they may see your good works and give glory to your Father who is in heaven"* (Matthew 5:16). Serving together deepens bonds and demonstrates the gospel to the world. Here are a few examples your group can do together:

- Serving at food banks or pregnancy centers.
- Partnering with schools for tutoring or projects.
- Visiting homebound members with cards, meals, or yard work.

Participation and Mission

True participation in small groups must move outward. As Jesus declared, *"As the Father has sent me, even so I am sending you"* (John 20:21). Groups that focus only inwardly may build fellowship but miss the mission. Healthy participation equips members to live as witnesses in their neighborhoods, workplaces, and communities.[104] Practical examples that encourage a mission focus include the following:

- Hospitality nights where each member invites an unchurched friend.

- Organizing service opportunities not only for relief (feeding the hungry) but also for relationship (sharing the gospel while serving).

- Participating together in church-wide outreach events, modeling mission as a lifestyle.

When participation extends beyond the group meeting, discipleship becomes holistic, head, heart, and hands working together in obedience to the Great Commission (Matthew 28:19–20).

Spiritual Gifts in Action

Participation gains depth when members discover and deploy their spiritual gifts. Paul describes these gifts as manifestations of the Spirit "for the common good" (1 Corinthians 12:7). A small group can serve as a laboratory for testing, affirming, and exercising gifts before members step

---

[104] See Donahue, *Building a Church of Small Groups*, 45–66; Gladen, *Small Groups with Purpose*, 23–52; Boren, *Missional Small Groups*, 71–95; Stanley and Willits, Creating Community, 29–54; Egli and Marable, *Small Groups, Big Impact*, 17–34; Anthony, "Small Groups in Protestant Churches," 257–72; Comiskey, "Value of Participating in Small Groups," 31–46.

into wider church leadership.[105] Here are some practical examples of how members use their spiritual gifts in action:

- A member with the gift of hospitality may naturally excel at hosting.

- A member with the gift of mercy may gravitate toward caring for needs within the group.

- A member with the gift of teaching might begin facilitating discussions under the leader's mentorship.

Rob Wegner and Brian Phipps remind us that gifts are not theoretical, they are tools for living out God's mission in daily life.[106] Helping members recognize and practice their gifts within the group affirms their identity and equips them for greater ministry impact.

Measuring Participation as Growth

When the subject of measuring participation comes up, we often focus on how many people are showing up. While numbers can represent growth, they are not the only measurement of participation. True growth in participation is more than counting heads, it is about spiritual fruit. As a leader, here are some questions to consider:

- Are members modeling Christlikeness more deeply?

---

[105] See Donahue, *Building a Church of Small Groups*, 45–66; Gladen, *Small Groups with Purpose*, 23–52; Boren, *Missional Small Groups*, 71–95; Stanley and Willits, Creating Community, 29–54; Egli and Marable, *Small Groups, Big Impact*, 17–34; Anthony, "Small Groups in Protestant Churches," 257–72; Comiskey, "Value of Participating in Small Groups," 31–46.

[106] Wegner and Phipps, Find Your Place, 25–27.

- Are apprentices being trained and deployed?
- Are visitors welcomed and engaged?
- Is the group serving beyond itself?

To evaluate whether participation is producing discipleship, consider the *Head–Heart–Hands Framework*. This three-fold lens ensures participation is not reduced to busyness but measured by transformation. Participation is the clearest sign that a group is alive and multiplying. A group where only the leader speaks is a lecture. A group where everyone shares, serves, and grows is a family.[107]

- **Head:** Are members learning biblical truth and articulating it in discussion?

- **Heart:** Are they growing in love, humility, and authenticity with one another?

- **Hands:** Are they serving within and beyond the group?

Common Pitfalls in Participation

Even well-meaning groups can easily slip into unhealthy patterns, such as allowing a few dominant voices to discourage others from engaging, mistaking busyness and activity for true discipleship and transformation, or treating participation as optional, something only for the 'keen' few rather than the calling of all. Wise leaders must guard against these tendencies

---

[107] See Donahue, *Building a Church of Small Groups*, 45–66; Gladen, *Small Groups with Purpose*, 23–52; Boren, *Missional Small Groups*, 71–95; Stanley and Willits, Creating Community, 29–54; Egli and Marable, *Small Groups, Big Impact*, 17–34; Anthony, "Small Groups in Protestant Churches," 257–72; Comiskey, "Value of Participating in Small Groups," 31–46.

by continually returning to the biblical vision of the body of Christ, where *"each part does its work"* (Ephesians 4:16).[108]

Conclusion

When participation thrives, small groups move from being leader-centered to Christ-centered communities. They cease to be just meetings and become movements—families of disciples who engage, serve, and multiply. Leaders who intentionally cultivate participation are not just teaching lessons; they are shaping disciples who will shape others.

Reflective Questions

1. Do I create space for members to contribute, or do I dominate discussion?

2. Am I raising up apprentices who can one day lead?

3. Are inactive members being pursued with love and prayer?

4. Is my group serving together beyond the meeting time?

---

[108] See Donahue, *Building a Church of Small Groups*, 45–66; Gladen, *Small Groups with Purpose*, 23–52; Boren, *Missional Small Groups*, 71–95; Stanley and Willits, Creating Community, 29–54; Egli and Marable, *Small Groups, Big Impact*, 17–34; Anthony, "Small Groups in Protestant Churches," 257–72; Comiskey, "Value of Participating in Small Groups," 31–46.

Chapter 7: Prayer

"The earnest prayer of a righteous person has great power as it is working." – James 5:16 (ESV)

Prayer is not filler between discussion questions. It is the engine of discipleship. When small groups pray deeply, they encounter God together, depend on His Spirit, and align their mission with His heart. Teaching, discussion, and fellowship are valuable, but prayer transforms a group from a gathering into a gospel movement. Jesus Himself declared, *"Apart from Me you can do nothing"* (John 15:5).

Why Prayer Matters

Prayer is not optional for the disciple of Jesus; it is essential. At its core, prayer is both communion with God and conformity to His will, drawing us into relationship while shaping us to reflect His purposes. Scripture repeatedly emphasizes the necessity of prayer, revealing four vital truths about why it matters.[109]

---

[109] See Elmer L. Towns, *How to Pray: What the Bible Teaches about Genuine, Effective Prayer* (Ventura, CA: Regal, 2006), 115–22; E. M. Bounds, *Power through Prayer* (Grand Rapids: Baker Book House, 1991), 25–30; Dietrich Bonhoeffer, *Life Together*, trans. John W. Doberstein (New York: Harper & Row, 1954), 84–87; D. A. Carson, *A Call to Spiritual Reformation: Priorities from Paul and His Prayers* (Grand Rapids: Baker Academic, 1992), 65–78; John Piper, *Let the Nations Be Glad! The Supremacy of God in Missions*, 3rd ed. (Grand Rapids: Baker Academic, 2010), 71–84; Charles H. Spurgeon, *Spurgeon on Prayer & Spiritual Warfare* (New Kensington, PA: Whitaker House, 1997), 43–46; Ken Braddy, "Why Prayer Must Be Central in Your Group," Ken Braddy Blog, Lifeway Christian Resources, May 14, 2020, https://kenbraddy.com/2020/05/14/why-prayer-must-be-central-in-your-group/; and Ed Stetzer and Eric Geiger, *Transformational Groups: Creating a New Scorecard for Groups* (Nashville: B&H, 2014), 151–65.

First, **prayer is commanded**. Paul exhorts believers to *"pray without ceasing"* (1 Thessalonians 5:17) and to "continue steadfastly in prayer, being watchful in it with thanksgiving" (Colossians 4:2). To neglect prayer is not simply to overlook a discipline—it is to neglect obedience to God's Word. Second, **prayer expresses dependence**. Jesus reminds us, *"Apart from me you can do nothing"* (John 15:5). When we pray, we confess our inability to accomplish God's work on our own and acknowledge our need for His Spirit to move. Third, **prayer aligns us with God's purposes**. In Gethsemane, Jesus prayed, *"Not my will, but yours, be done"* (Luke 22:42). True prayer is not about bending God to our desires but allowing Him to reshape our hearts to match His. Finally, **prayer unleashes God's power**. The early church advanced on its knees: they prayed and were filled with the Spirit (Acts 4:31), they prayed and God sent workers into the harvest (Matthew 9:38), and they prayed and saw miraculous deliverance, as when Peter's chains fell off in prison (Acts 12:5–7).

Prayer, then, is not a filler between activities but the very engine of discipleship and mission. It is how believers remain connected to Christ, empowered by the Spirit, and aligned with the Father's will, fueling both personal transformation and kingdom advance. The "why" of prayer is clear: without prayer, disciples dry up; with prayer, disciples grow and groups multiply. As Oswald Chambers observed, "Prayer does not fit us for the greater work; prayer is the greater work."[110]

The Theology of Prayer

Prayer is the believer's lifeline to God, the natural response of faith, and the essential posture of dependence. Prayer is not

---

[110] Oswald Chambers, My Utmost for His Highest (Grand Rapids: Discovery House, 1992), 120.

optional—it is commanded (1 Thessalonians 5:17), modeled by Jesus (Luke 5:16), and expected of God's people (Matthew 6:9–13).

The first Christians were marked by prayer. Luke records, *"And they devoted themselves…to the prayers"* (Acts 2:42). Their identity as disciples was inseparable from their devotion to calling on the Lord. When Peter was imprisoned, the church gathered in a home to pray earnestly (Acts 12:12). When the apostles faced threats, they lifted their voices together and prayed for boldness (Acts 4:23–31). Prayer was not an accessory to their life together; it was central. Their prayer was urgent, unified, and expectant.

Corporate and personal prayer are two lungs of one life. Jesus prayed alone (Luke 5:16) and with others (Luke 9:28; Acts 1:14). Small groups should breathe with both lungs, personal prayer that fuels corporate prayer, and corporate prayer that trains personal prayer.

Another component in the theology of prayer is praying in Jesus' name. This is not merely a formula to be repeated but a posture of the heart, asking in alignment with His person, purposes, and promises (John 14:13–14; 16:23–24). To pray in His name is to surrender our will to His, trusting that what we ask is both rooted in His character and directed toward His glory.[111]

---

[111] See Towns, *How to Pray*, 115–22; Bounds, *Power through Prayer*, 25–30; Bonhoeffer, *Life Together*, 84–87; Carson, *A Call to Spiritual Reformation*, 65–78; Piper, *Let the Nations Be Glad!*, 71–84; Spurgeon, *Spurgeon on Prayer & Spiritual Warfare*, 43–46; Braddy, "Why Prayer Must Be Central"; Stetzer and Geiger, *Transformational Groups*, 151–65.

The Foundation of Spiritual Power

Prayer is not an optional add-on to group life, it is the very lifeblood of Christian community. While it is important for a small group to set aside time to pray together during gatherings, prayer must not be confined to that one window. Healthy groups cultivate rhythms of prayer throughout the week. This can be as simple as sending a midweek text update, sharing an urgent need by email, or setting aside a specific time where members stop and pray for one another wherever they are. These practices remind us that prayer is not bound to a meeting but woven into the daily fabric of our relationships.

One of the greatest barriers to authentic prayer is fear of vulnerability. We hesitate to be open about our struggles, sins, or doubts. Yet Scripture calls us not only to pray but also to confess and intercede (James 5:16). Real community is built when members feel safe enough to bring both their praises and their pain before God together. Dietrich Bonhoeffer once observed, "A Christian fellowship lives and exists by the intercession of its members for one another, or it collapses."[112] Prayer binds hearts in unity, tears down walls of isolation, and builds spiritual family.

Our prayers should be both wide and deep. It is good to pray for the sick, for those carrying heavy burdens, and for daily needs. But the scope of prayer must stretch beyond ourselves. We are called to intercede for the lost (Romans 10:1), to cry out for revival in our city (Jeremiah 29:7), and to pray for God's kingdom to advance across the world (Matthew 6:10). When groups lift their eyes beyond their own needs and

---

[112] Dietrich Bonhoeffer, Life Together, trans. John W. Doberstein (New York: Harper & Row, 1954), 86.

plead for God's mission, they are reminded that they are part of something far bigger than themselves.

Prayer should also be intentional, uplifting, and challenging. Intentional, in that it is woven naturally but purposefully into group life. Uplifting, in that it strengthens weary hearts and encourages the faint. Challenging, in that it pushes us to step beyond comfortable petitions and into bold intercession that expects God to move.

Without prayer, small groups risk becoming social clubs or study circles, places of connection but not transformation. With prayer, they become Spirit-filled families where burdens are carried, lives are changed, and God's power is displayed. Prayer is the difference between natural outcomes and supernatural fruit.

Charles Spurgeon once said, "Prayer moves the arm that moves the world."[113] Every awakening, every mission advance, every transformed life begins in prayer. When groups commit themselves to seek God in honest, fervent, and faith-filled prayer, they position themselves to experience His presence and power in ways that far exceed human effort.[114]

---

[113] Charles H. Spurgeon, Twelve Sermons on Prayer (Pasadena, TX: Pilgrim Publications, 1971), 24.

[114] See Towns, *How to Pray*, 115–22; Bounds, *Power through Prayer*, 25–30; Bonhoeffer, *Life Together*, 84–87; Carson, *A Call to Spiritual Reformation*, 65–78; Piper, *Let the Nations Be Glad!*, 71–84; Spurgeon, *Spurgeon on Prayer & Spiritual Warfare*, 43–46; Braddy, "Why Prayer Must Be Central"; Stetzer and Geiger, *Transformational Groups*, 151–65.

A Vulnerability Ladder (to normalize James 5:16)

1. Start with praises and simple needs.
2. Share one pressure from the week.
3. Name one sin to resist this week.
4. Invite one partner to follow-up midweek.
5. Celebrate grace received and growth observed

The Leader's Private Prayer Life

Before leaders can lead in prayer, they must live in prayer. E.M. Bounds famously wrote, "The church is looking for better methods; God is looking for better men—men of prayer."[115] Leaders who neglect prayer may lead busy groups but not powerful ones.

Paul modeled this when he wrote to the Colossians, *"We have not ceased to pray for you, asking that you may be filled with the knowledge of his will"* (Colossians 1:9). Prayer was not a ministry accessory for Paul, it was the very heart of his ministry. Here are two effective methods of prayer that I have used as a small group leader to help you be intentional in your personal prayer life for your small group.

A 5-Day Intercession Map (repeat weekly):

- **Monday:** Names A–F (spiritual growth: Ephesians 3:16–19)
- **Tuesday:** G–L (temptations & holiness: 1 Thessalonians 4:3–8)

---

[115] E.M. Bounds, Power Through Prayer (Grand Rapids: Baker, 1991), 7.

- **Wednesday:** M–R (suffering & comfort: 2 Corinthians 1:3–7)
- **Thursday:** S–Z (wisdom & calling: Colossians 1:9–12)
- **Friday:** FRAN list (Friends/Relatives/Associates/ Neighbors—salvation & boldness: Romans 10:1; Acts 4:29)[116]

Elmer Towns outlines five ways teachers should pray for their groups:[117]

- Pray for a teachable spirit. Ask God to soften hearts.
- Pray for the Spirit's teaching ministry. Depend on Him to do what human words cannot.
- Pray for guidance in lesson preparation. Ask God to illuminate truth for the moment.
- Pray for those in your class. Lift each member by name.
- Pray for class growth. Not only numerical growth, but maturity in Christ.

Leaders who carry members to the throne of grace privately will see power publicly. Quiet intercession shapes the heart before it steers the room; names prayed over in secret become the names God strengthens in plain sight. Establish a simple weekly rhythm, Scripture-fed prayer, a rotating name list, and

---

[116] The "FRAN List" (Friends/Relatives/Associates/Neighbors) is a commonly used evangelism tool promoted in various church and ministry training contexts, including the North American Mission Board and other evangelistic resources. It emphasizes intentional prayer and gospel witness toward those within one's relational network. See North American Mission Board, Evangelism Resources (Alpharetta, GA: NAMB, 2010–), https:// www.namb.net/evangelism/.

[117] Elmer Towns, What Every Sunday School Teacher Should Know (Grand Rapids: Baker, 2001), 49–51.

brief check-ins and entrust the outcomes to the Spirit. When leaders kneel in hidden places, groups rise in visible fruit.[118]

Corporate Prayer in the Group

Prayer should be woven into the fabric of group meetings, not tacked on at the end. Jesus warned against hypocritical, performance-driven prayer (Matthew 6:5–6) and against *"empty phrases"* that lacked sincerity (Matthew 6:7). True prayer flows from humility before the Father and confidence in His will.[119] The following are some examples of on-ramps for the hesitant:

- Invite one-sentence prayers.
- Use Scripture prompts (e.g., each person prays a phrase from Psalm 23).
- Pair-and-share: 2–3 minutes in pairs before whole-group prayer.

Group prayer is a powerful time of connection with God and with one another, but it thrives best when guided by clear guardrails. Four key principles can help ensure that prayer remains balanced, Holy Spirit-led, and accessible to everyone. First, practice **confidentiality**, what is shared in prayer must stay within the group, creating a safe place for honesty and vulnerability. Second, encourage **brevity** by modeling many short, sincere prayers rather than a few lengthy ones, so that everyone has the opportunity to participate. Third, exercise

---

[118] See Towns, *How to Pray*, 115–22; Bounds, *Power through Prayer*, 25–30; Bonhoeffer, *Life Together*, 84–87; Carson, *A Call to Spiritual Reformation*, 65–78; Piper, *Let the Nations Be Glad!*, 71–84; Spurgeon, *Spurgeon on Prayer & Spiritual Warfare*, 43–46; Braddy, "Why Prayer Must Be Central"; Stetzer and Geiger, *Transformational Groups*, 151–65.

[119] Martin Luther, *A Simple Way to Pray* (1522).

charity by resisting the urge to fix problems or offer mini-sermons through prayer; instead, focus on lifting one another before the Lord with compassion. Finally, prioritize **safety** by keeping confessions of sin general in mixed settings while allowing more specific confession in same-gender breakouts where trust can be deeper. When these guardrails are consistently practiced, group prayer becomes not only orderly but also deeply unifying, helping participants experience God's presence together in meaningful ways.

One practical way to cultivate corporate prayer in small groups is by using a simple framework that provides both structure and freedom. Many groups find that having a brief liturgy gives everyone a chance to participate without feeling overwhelmed or lost. A 10-minute prayer rhythm, rotated weekly among group members, can help the whole group experience prayer together in a balanced way:

- **Adoration (1 min):** Speak out one-word attributes of God.
- **Thanksgiving (2 min):** Offer rapid-fire prayers of gratitude.
- **Confession (2 min):** Begin in silence, then move to one-sentence prayers of confession.
- **Intercession (3 min):** Lift up two or three pressing needs.
- **Mission (2 min):** Name lost friends and upcoming gospel opportunities.

This simple guide keeps prayer from becoming routine while encouraging everyone to engage. When members pray aloud, ownership increases, faith deepens, and community grows (James 5:16). Most importantly, this rhythm reinforces the truth that every believer is called to minister through prayer, not merely observe from the sidelines.[120]

Prayer for the Lost, for Each Other, and for Mission

Left unchecked, group prayer can shrink to the crises inside our own circle. While praying for health needs is loving and right, leaders should widen the lens toward God's name, kingdom, and will (Matthew 6:9–10), interceding for the lost, for gospel opportunities and boldness, for laborers and leaders, for our city and authorities, for justice and the poor, and for the nations and the persecuted church (1 Timothy 2:1–4; Colossians 4:2–4; Acts 4:29; Matthew 9:37–38; Hebrews 13:3). To help your group pray bigger, consider:[121]

- **Pray for unbelieving friends by name:** Paul prayed earnestly for his fellow Jews to be saved (Romans 10:1).

- **Pray for missionaries and global needs:** This stretches the group's perspective beyond its walls.

- **Pray for courage to live on mission:** The early believers prayed for boldness to proclaim Christ (Acts 4:29).

[120] See Towns, *How to Pray*, 115–22; Bounds, *Power through Prayer*, 25–30; Bonhoeffer, *Life Together*, 84–87; Carson, *A Call to Spiritual Reformation*, 65–78; Piper, *Let the Nations Be Glad!*, 71–84; Spurgeon, *Spurgeon on Prayer & Spiritual Warfare*, 43–46; Braddy, "Why Prayer Must Be Central"; Stetzer and Geiger, *Transformational Groups*, 151–65.

[121] See Towns, *How to Pray*, 115–22; Bounds, *Power through Prayer*, 25–30; Bonhoeffer, *Life Together*, 84–87; Carson, *A Call to Spiritual Reformation*, 65–78; Piper, *Let the Nations Be Glad!*, 71–84; Spurgeon, *Spurgeon on Prayer & Spiritual Warfare*, 43–46; Braddy, "Why Prayer Must Be Central"; Stetzer and Geiger, *Transformational Groups*, 151–65.

As David Francis notes, even a simple prayer for a neighbor can be the first step toward evangelism.[122] Groups that pray for the lost often see God open unexpected doors for witness. Here is a simple model for group prayer:

- **Pray Upward (Worship & Thanksgiving)**
  Begin by lifting your eyes to God. Thank Him for who He is and what He has done. Pray Scripture back to Him in adoration. This centers the group's focus on God's character before moving to requests (Psalm 100:4; Hebrews 13:15).

- **Pray Inward (Intercession for the Group)**
  Turn inward to the needs of the group itself. Share personal requests, confess struggles, and pray for one another's growth in Christ. This step builds transparency, accountability, and care within the group (James 5:16; Galatians 6:2).

- **Pray Outward (Mission & the Lost)**
  Finally, look outward together. Pray for unsaved friends and family by name, for the city and community, and for global missions. Ask God to use your group as a light for the gospel (Romans 10:1; Matthew 28:19–20).

This rhythm helps groups avoid drifting into self-focused prayer. It balances upward worship, inward care, and outward mission—aligning the group's heart with God's purposes.

---

[122] David Francis, Missionary Sunday School (Nashville: LifeWay, 2011), 24 .

Prayer as a Discipleship Practice

Prayer forms disciples, not just meets needs. J.C. Ryle wrote, "Just as the first sign of life in an infant when born into the world is the act of breathing, so the first act of men and women when they are born again is praying."[123]

Prayer is not only an expression of faith but also a method of discipleship. Just as leaders teach others how to study Scripture or share their faith, they can also teach people how to pray. Many believers—especially new ones—have never been shown what prayer looks like beyond offering thanks before meals or asking for help in times of crisis. Small groups provide a natural environment to model prayer, guide others in practicing it, and multiply prayer as a shared rhythm of discipleship. A practical rhythm to teach and model is:[124]

- **Upward (Adoration):** Directing prayer to God's character and worth. Example: "Father, You are faithful and near; Your mercies are new this morning." (Psalm 100; Hebrews 13:15)

- **Inward (Intercession/Confession):** Bringing personal needs and weaknesses to the Lord. Example: "Spirit, strengthen James to endure his trial; guard his tongue and heart." (James 5:16; Galatians 6:2)

---

[123] J.C. Ryle, A Call to Prayer (Carlisle: Banner of Truth, 2012), 8 .

[124] See Towns, *How to Pray*, 115–22; Bounds, *Power through Prayer*, 25–30; Bonhoeffer, *Life Together*, 84–87; Carson, *A Call to Spiritual Reformation*, 65–78; Piper, *Let the Nations Be Glad!*, 71–84; Spurgeon, *Spurgeon on Prayer & Spiritual Warfare*, 43–46; Braddy, "Why Prayer Must Be Central"; Stetzer and Geiger, *Transformational Groups*, 151–65.

- **Outward (Mission):** Praying for the lost and for gospel opportunities. Example: "Lord, save Maria; open doors for us to speak of Christ with clarity." (Romans 10:1; Colossians 4:3–4)

These movements can be introduced in group settings as methods of prayer. Leaders can assign one "direction" to different members during prayer time, or walk through all three together as a rhythm. Over time, participants learn that prayer is not random but can be structured in ways that form their faith.

Another helpful method is what Donald Whitney suggests praying through Scripture, especially the Psalms, line by line: "Simply go through the passage, talking to God about whatever comes to mind as you read the text."[125] This method not only teaches believers how to pray but also aligns their prayers with God's Word, shaping their desires and requests according to Scripture.

By modeling these methods consistently, leaders transform prayer time from a quick ritual into a discipleship practice—showing group members how to adore God, confess honestly, intercede for one another, and plead for the lost. Over time, even those who once said, "I don't know how to pray," can grow into disciples who pray with depth, boldness, and joy.[126]

---

[125] Donald S. Whitney, Praying the Bible (Wheaton: Crossway, 2015), 27 .

[126] See Towns, *How to Pray*, 115–22; Bounds, *Power through Prayer*, 25–30; Bonhoeffer, *Life Together*, 84–87; Carson, *A Call to Spiritual Reformation*, 65–78; Piper, *Let the Nations Be Glad!*, 71–84; Spurgeon, *Spurgeon on Prayer & Spiritual Warfare*, 43–46; Braddy, "Why Prayer Must Be Central"; Stetzer and Geiger, *Transformational Groups*, 151–65.

Missional Prayer: Walking and Witnessing

Prayer doesn't stop when the chairs are stacked; it spills into streets, schedules, and screens. Scripture calls us to pray "at all times" (Ephesians 6:18), to seek our city's good (Jeremiah 29:7), and to watch for open doors for the gospel (Colossians 4:2–4). With that vision, leaders can help groups carry intercession beyond the living room or classroom—into daily rhythms, shared spaces, and missional moments. Practically, leaders can guide their groups in:

- **Prayer Walking:** Walking neighborhoods, observing needs, and interceding for families, schools, and leaders. Even those with physical limitations can participate through map prayer or prayer drives (see Appendix 6).

- **Evangelistic Intercession:** Asking coworkers, neighbors, or strangers, "How can I pray for you this week?" Prayer often opens doors for gospel conversations before a sermon is ever heard.

When prayer goes missional, groups begin to see themselves as outposts of the kingdom. Intercession widens to include neighbors and nations, and petitions become plans, meals shared, invitations extended, and acts of mercy scheduled (Colossians 4:2–6; 1 Timothy 2:1–4). Depending on the Spirit, we ask for boldness and clarity, then speak and serve in Jesus' name (Acts 4:29–31; 1 Peter 3:15). Sent by the risen Lord (John 20:21), we expect God to open doors and open hearts, trusting that our small circle can shine as a city on a hill (Matthew 5:14–16).[127]

Guarding Against Prayer Drift

One danger is reducing prayer to health updates. While physical needs matter and we should pray for the sick (James 5:14–16), our intercession must be bigger than illness and appointments. To align with the Lord's Prayer and the church's mission, leaders should guide prayer toward:

- Spiritual growth and holiness.
- Boldness in gospel witness.
- Healing and reconciliation in relationships.
- Wisdom for leadership and decision-making (Ephesians 6:18–20; Colossians 4:2–4).

Balanced prayer reflects biblical priorities and trains believers to see the world through the lens of God's kingdom. Groups don't usually abandon prayer; they drift from Scripture-fed, many-voiced intercession to long updates, few speakers, and narrow horizons. Scripture calls us to *"continue steadfastly in prayer"* (Colossians 4:2), to pray *"at all times in the Spirit"* (Ephesians 6:18), and to devote ourselves to prayer together (Acts 2:42). *The Troubleshooting Matrix Chart* on the following page is a practical dashboard to help you diagnose what you're seeing and act quickly so your group's prayer stays

---

[127] See Towns, *How to Pray*, 115–22; Bounds, *Power through Prayer*, 25–30; Bonhoeffer, *Life Together*, 84–87; Carson, *A Call to Spiritual Reformation*, 65–78; Piper, *Let the Nations Be Glad!*, 71–84; Spurgeon, *Spurgeon on Prayer & Spiritual Warfare*, 43–46; Braddy, "Why Prayer Must Be Central"; Stetzer and Geiger, *Transformational Groups*, 151–65.

earnest, participatory, and mission-facing.[128] Here are four steps on how to use *The Troubleshooting Matrix Chart*:

1. Name the problem you're noticing (e.g., only a few pray, requests consume the time).

2. Identify the likely cause from the middle column.

3. Choose one simple fix (right column), assign an owner, and put it on the calendar for the next meeting.

4. Pray, implement, review in one week—then keep what bears fruit and try the next small adjustment.

Leader's Charge: Keep prayer Scripture-fed, short and sincere, many-voiced, and mission-oriented. Protect confidentiality, model vulnerability, and always end by praying for the lost and for bold gospel opportunities.

---

[128] See Towns, *How to Pray*, 115–22; Bounds, *Power through Prayer*, 25–30; Bonhoeffer, *Life Together*, 84–87; Carson, *A Call to Spiritual Reformation*, 65–78; Piper, *Let the Nations Be Glad!*, 71–84; Spurgeon, *Spurgeon on Prayer & Spiritual Warfare*, 43–46; Braddy, "Why Prayer Must Be Central"; Stetzer and Geiger, *Transformational Groups*, 151–65.

Troubleshooting Matrix Chart

Problem	Likely Cause	Simple Fix
Long request time, little prayer	Sharing eclipses praying	5-minute timer for requests; pray as needs are named
Awkward silence	Fear of not "saying" it right	Use one-sentence prompts; pair-and-share first
Only a few pray	Dominating voices	Leader goes last; call on 2-3 by name (optional participation)
Only health needs	Narrow horizon	Keep FRAN cards visible; always end with mission
Confession scarce	Low trust	Same-gender breakouts monthly; confidentiality covenant

Conclusion: The Power Behind the Mission

When prayer becomes central, small groups stop being natural gatherings and become supernatural communities. Prayer is not just part of the meeting — it is the power behind the mission.

Prayerless groups will produce activity, but prayer-filled groups will produce fruit that lasts. As Jesus promised, *"If you abide in me, and my words abide in you, ask whatever you wish, and it will be done for you. By this my Father is glorified, that you bear much fruit and so prove to be my disciples"* (John 15:7–8).

Reflective Questions

1. Do I model prayer as dependence on God, or as a formality?

2. Does my group's prayer life extend beyond physical needs to spiritual transformation and mission?

3. Are members actively participating in prayer, or am I doing it all?

4. Have I prayed this week for God to use my group to reach the lost?

Conclusion to Part 2

Preparation, Presentation, Participation, and Prayer are not four disconnected skills but four interwoven strands that form a single cord of effective discipleship. Preparation anchors the leader in God's Word and purposes (2 Timothy 2:15), which in turn shapes faithful Presentation—clear, humble handling of Scripture so people *"understand the reading"* (Nehemiah 8:8). Thoughtful Presentation then invites real Participation, where the body *"builds itself up in love"* as each member contributes (Ephesians 4:15–16; 1 Corinthians 12:7). And Participation is deepened and directed through Prayer—the church's lifeline to God's power and presence (Acts 2:42; James 5:16; Philippians 4:6–7).

Held together, these four principles transform small groups from meetings into movements. We move beyond information transfer to Spirit-empowered formation, beyond passive attendance to shared ministry, beyond private devotion to public witness. Jesus' words remind us that apart from Him we can do nothing (John 15:5), yet in His commission we are sent to make disciples who obey all He commanded (Matthew 28:18–20). Groups that prepare well, present Scripture faithfully, cultivate broad participation, and pray earnestly will naturally look outward in mission (Acts 1:8) and multiply leaders who can teach others also (2 Timothy 2:2).

As you turn to Part 3—Practices for Healthy Groups, you will put this framework to work:

- **Chapter 8:** Clarifying the Purpose (why your group exists)
- **Chapter 9**: Practical Organization (how your group functions)

- **Chapter 10:** Pastoral Care (how your group loves)
- **Chapter 11:** Multiplication (how your group reproduces)

With these practices, the four strands will be woven into the weekly life of your group—so that Christ is formed in His people and His mission advances through them.

Part 3: Practices

Chapter 8: Clarifying the Purpose

"And they devoted themselves to the apostles' teaching and the fellowship, to the breaking of bread and the prayers...And the Lord added to their number day by day those who were being saved." — (Acts 2:42, 47, ESV)

The Importance of Clarifying Purpose

Every small group begins with a spark of energy. New faces gather, relationships form, and there is excitement about what God might do. Yet over time, groups can lose their way. A group that began as a disciple-making community may drift into something far less intentional, a weekly social club, an inward-focused clique, or simply a routine gathering with little mission. The difference between a growing, disciple-making group and a stagnant one often comes down to this: clarity of purpose. Without a shared "why," a group drifts. With a clear and revisited purpose, a group thrives.

The early church in Acts 2 provides the model: they devoted themselves to the Word, to fellowship, to prayer, and to mission. These anchors shaped their identity. The same must hold true for today's small groups.

Avoiding Drift

Drift is natural. Unless leaders consistently re-center their groups, subtle shifts occur. Fellowship becomes the focus while mission fades. Study becomes academic rather than transformative. Prayer becomes routine rather than Spirit-led.

Fellowship, study, and prayer are all good—but they must not replace the mission of Christ. As Jesus said, *"Go therefore and make disciples of all nations"* (Matthew 28:19). Small groups are disciple-making outposts, not cul-de-sacs of comfort. Leaders must regularly ask: Is our group growing as disciples? Are we helping one another follow Jesus more faithfully? Are we engaged in God's mission?

Revisiting Mission and Vision

Paul never assumed churches remembered their mission. He wrote frequent reminders, *"To write the same things to you is no trouble to me and is safe for you"* (Philippians 3:1). Similarly, Peter urged, *"I intend always to remind you of these qualities…to stir you up by way of reminder"* (2 Peter 1:12–13).

Healthy small group leaders follow this biblical pattern. They remind their groups: "We exist to grow as disciples of Jesus and to multiply disciples through relationships." This vision should not be assumed; it must be repeated, celebrated, and lived.[129]

The Three-Fold Mission of Small Groups

Every healthy small group must hold three priorities in tension, **Upward, Inward, and Outward**. These are not optional add-ons but biblical essentials that shape the mission of Christian community. When a group leans too heavily on study, fellowship, or service alone, it quickly becomes lopsided. A balanced group embraces all three, growing in

---

[129] Breen and Cockram, *BDC*, 47; Putman, *RLD*, 90; Donahue, *Life-Changing Small Groups*, 115; Bonhoeffer, *Life Together*, 27.

Christlikeness, living in authentic community, and engaging the world with the gospel. Together these priorities create a holistic picture of discipleship that reflects the mission of Jesus and the design of the church.

The **Upward** priority is about growing in Christlikeness. At the heart of every small group is the call to pursue Christ together. Growth is not measured simply by knowledge gained but by lives transformed through God's Word. As Paul wrote, *"All Scripture is breathed out by God...that the man of God may be complete, equipped for every good work"* (2 Timothy 3:16–17, ESV). This upward focus keeps Scripture central and presses groups to ask, How does this passage call us to live differently? and How does it lead us to worship Christ more fully? James warns, *"Be doers of the word, and not hearers only"* (James 1:22). In short, the upward dimension reminds us that discipleship is not about information but transformation through obedience.

The **Inward** priority calls believers to live in authentic community. Christianity is never a solo journey; God places His people together so they might bear one another's burdens, rejoice in victories, and endure hardships side by side. Paul wrote, *"Bear one another's burdens, and so fulfill the law of Christ"* (Galatians 6:2), and he urged believers to *"rejoice with those who rejoice, weep with those who weep"* (Romans 12:15). A healthy group is not defined merely by weekly meetings but by shared life, celebrating birthdays, grieving losses, and cheering victories over sin. This depth of care reflects the love Jesus spoke of when He said, *"By this all people will know that you are my disciples, if you have love for one another"* (John 13:35). Inwardly focused groups become safe places where people are known, prayed for, and supported.

147

The **Outward** priority compels groups to engage the world. Small groups are not meant to become holy huddles but training grounds for mission and launching pads for ministry. Jesus' Great Commission is clear: "Go therefore and make disciples of all nations..." (Matthew 28:19–20). Healthy groups encourage members to pray for unbelieving friends, share Christ in daily life, and support local and global missions. Jesus also said, *"Let your light shine before others, so that they may see your good works and give glory to your Father who is in heaven"* (Matthew 5:16). This outward focus ensures groups avoid turning in on themselves and instead exist as outposts of the kingdom of God—making Christ visible through both word and deed. In this way, small groups live out the full mission of the church by reaching up in worship, reaching in through community, and reaching out in mission.[130]

Holding All Three in Balance

A small group that emphasizes only Upward becomes a Bible study with no mission. One that focuses only Inward risks becoming a social club. One that emphasizes only Outward may become a service team with no spiritual depth. Biblical small groups weave all three together.

- They **look up** in worship and obedience.

- They **look in** with love and community.

- They **look out** in mission and service.

---

[130] Breen and Cockram, *BDC*, 47; Putman, *RLD*, 90; Donahue, *Life-Changing Small Groups*, 115; Bonhoeffer, *Life Together*, 27.

When these three are held together, the group reflects the full mission of Christ and embodies the life of the church as God intended.

Tools for Clarifying Purpose

Practical tools can help leaders guard against drift and keep the mission of the small group at the forefront. To ensure members remain focused on the group's purpose, leaders should intentionally use clear and consistent practices. Here are a few practical tools I have found effective in clarifying the purpose of small groups for their members.[131]

- **Purpose Statement:** A short, memorable phrase summarizing why the group exists. Example small group statement: "We gather to know God, grow together, and make disciples who change the world."

- **Accountability Check-ins:** Periodically ask the small group: "Are we still focused on our mission? Where do we need realignment?"

- **Evaluation Rhythms:** Every few months, dedicate a meeting to reflection: What is working well? What is missing? Where is God leading us?

- **Mission Reminder Practices:** Begin each gathering with a 30-second restatement of the group's purpose. Post it on group texts or email updates.

---

[131] Breen and Cockram, *BDC*, 47; Putman, *RLD*, 90; Donahue, *Life-Changing Small Groups*, 115; Bonhoeffer, *Life Together*, 27.

Practical Tool: Mission Check Card

- Are we growing Upward? _____
- Are we loving Inward? _____
- Are we reaching Outward? _____

If any are missing, it's time to recalibrate.

Aligning with the Church's Mission

Small groups do not exist in isolation; they are living expressions of the church's larger disciple-making mission. When groups are aligned with the church, they become an extension of its vision rather than a separate entity. This alignment ensures that teaching and study reinforce the church's overall direction and priorities, providing consistency in doctrine and practice. Service projects flow out of the church's mission and complement, rather than compete with, broader ministry initiatives, strengthening the impact of both. In addition, small groups are called to pray faithfully for pastors, missionaries, and the church body as a whole, recognizing that they are part of something greater than themselves. In this way, groups remain tethered to the church's mission and contribute to a unified witness of the gospel in the community and beyond.

Ephesians 4 and 1 Corinthians 12 remind us that the church is one body with many parts, working together for growth and maturity in Christ (Ephesians 4:15–16; 1 Corinthians 12). When small groups intentionally align with the larger body of the church, both are strengthened and unified in purpose. Ask yourself: Is your small group aligned with your local church's mission? Take time to talk with your pastor and examine your church's disciple-making pathway. Together, discuss practical ways your group can better align with and support the mission of the local church of which you are a member.[132]

Avoiding Mission Drift

Some groups unintentionally distort their identity by narrowing their focus too much in one direction. **Social-only groups** emphasize fellowship but neglect discipleship, creating warm friendships without spiritual growth. **Study-only groups** pursue knowledge yet fail to put God's Word into practice, producing information without obedience. **Service-only groups** are quick to act but risk losing sight of worship, serving out of duty rather than devotion. A healthy small group resists these distortions by asking regularly, "Are we balancing our life together upward toward God, inward toward one another, and outward toward the world?" This rhythm ensures that fellowship, discipleship, and mission remain integrated, keeping the group aligned with God's design for His people.[133]

Conclusion: Purpose Fuels Multiplication

Clarifying and revisiting purpose keeps small groups from drifting and empowers them to multiply. Groups without purpose wander; groups with purpose reproduce disciples.

---

[132] Breen and Cockram, *BDC*, 47; Putman, *RLD*, 90; Donahue, *Life-Changing Small Groups*, 115; Bonhoeffer, *Life Together*, 27.

[133] Breen and Cockram, *BDC*, 47; Putman, *RLD*, 90; Donahue, *Life-Changing Small Groups*, 115; Bonhoeffer, *Life Together*, 27.

Paul's challenge to Timothy sets the trajectory, *"What you have heard from me…entrust to faithful men, who will be able to teach others also"* (2 Timothy 2:2). That is the heartbeat of small groups: not to sit in comfort, but to multiply disciples who make disciples. When groups clarify purpose, they become more than gatherings. They become movements of mission, outposts of God's kingdom advancing His glory in the world.

Reflection Questions

1. Can I articulate the purpose of my group in one sentence?

2. Does our group regularly revisit and restate our mission?

3. Are we balanced in growing Upward, Inward, and Outward?

4. In what ways does our group align with the mission of our church?

5. Where might we be drifting from our purpose?

Chapter 9: Practical Organization

"But all things should be done decently and in order." – 1
Corinthians 14:40 (ESV)

Why Organization Matters

Spiritual purpose fuels the group, but practical organization
sustains it. Organization in a small group is not about control; it
is about creating reproducible rhythms that free people to
thrive. Scripture affirms this balance, *"All things should be
done decently and in order"* (1 Corinthians 14:40). Paul left
Titus in Crete *"to put what remained into order"* (Titus 1:5),
and Moses learned from Jethro to structure care so that people
were truly shepherded (Exodus 18:17–23). Healthy systems
don't stifle the Spirit; they steward the mission.

When groups lack structure, care often suffers. Guests can
slip through unnoticed, absentees can be forgotten, and leaders
can burn out under the weight of carrying everything alone.
Disorganization is not neutral, it quietly undermines disciple-
making. In contrast, when systems are simple and consistent,
people feel seen, leaders are freed to focus on shepherding, and
the mission of making disciples moves forward with clarity.
Organization is not busywork; it is the framework that keeps
people cared for and discipleship on track.

A Biblical Foundation for Organization

I admit that organization comes naturally to me, it is how
God has wired me. Yet I also know it doesn't come easily to
everyone. Some even fear that structure somehow limits the
work of the Holy Spirit. But Scripture teaches the opposite:

preparation and order create the environment where the Spirit works powerfully. Paul reminded the Corinthians that *"all things should be done decently and in order"* (1 Corinthians 14:40), not to quench the Spirit, but to build up the body. I have personally seen moments when the Spirit redirected a message or shifted the flow of a meeting, and He used the very framework of preparation to do it. Being organized does not schedule out the Spirit; it simply positions us to be faithful stewards of the opportunities He brings. With this in mind, let us look at a biblical foundation for organization that strengthens the church.[134]

A biblical foundation for organization reminds us that structure in the church is never about bureaucracy for its own sake but about strengthening Christ's body. **Order serves edification**. Paul ties order directly to the building up of the church: *"Let all things be done for building up...but all things should be done decently and in order"* (1 Corinthians 14:26, 40). Organization is not about rigid control or efficiency alone but about creating an environment where worship is clear, disciples are formed, and the whole body is encouraged.

---

[134] See Steve Gladen, *Small Groups with Purpose: How to Create Healthy Communities* (Grand Rapids: Baker Books, 2011); Bill Donahue, *Leading Life-Changing Small Groups*, 3rd ed. (Downers Grove, IL: InterVarsity Press, 2012); Andy Stanley and Bill Willits, *Creating Community: Five Keys to Building a Small Group Culture* (Sisters, OR: Multnomah, 2004); Larry Kreider and Jimmy Seibert, *House to House: Growing Healthy Small Groups and House Churches in the 21st Century* (Shippensburg, PA: Destiny Image, 2000); Ken Braddy, "Six Keys to Organizing and Leading Sunday School Classes and Groups," Lifeway Research Blog, April 15, 2020, https://kenbraddy.com; Rick Howerton, *A Different Kind of Tribe: Embracing the New Small Group Dynamic* (Nashville: Serendipity House, 2009); Joel Comiskey, *How to Lead a Great Cell Group Meeting...So People Want to Come Back* (Moreno Valley, CA: CCS Publishing, 2010); Greg Ogden, *Transforming Discipleship: Making Disciples a Few at a Time*, rev. ed. (Downers Grove, IL: InterVarsity Press, 2016).

Shared service equips the saints. In Ephesians 4:11–12, Paul explains that Christ gave leaders to equip His people for the work of ministry. Organization clarifies responsibilities so that leaders can train, and members can serve in ways that use their God-given gifts. Without structure, many remain uncertain of their role; with structure, the whole body works together to accomplish the mission of God.

Multiplication requires planning. Jesus modeled intentional organization by sending His disciples out in pairs (Luke 10:1), calling an inner circle to deeper investment (Mark 3:14), and commissioning them to make disciples who would, in turn, disciple others (Matthew 28:19–20; 2 Timothy 2:2). Growth in the kingdom is never accidental; it is prayerfully and purposefully cultivated. Organization ensures that multiplication is sustainable and reproducible across generations.

Finally, **practical systems protect care.** In Acts 6:1–7, the apostles faced a crisis when widows were being neglected in food distribution. Their solution was to appoint servants to oversee the task, ensuring that no one was overlooked. As a result, *"the word of God continued to increase, and the number of the disciples multiplied greatly" (Acts 6:7).* Good organization protects the vulnerable, frees leaders to focus on their calling, and enables the church to grow in both faithfulness and fruitfulness.

At the heart of leading a small group is the balance between faithful preparation and Holy Spirit-filled flexibility. Scripture calls us to order, stewardship, and intentionality, yet it also reminds us that the Spirit moves as He wills (John 3:8). Our planning is not opposed to His presence, it is the very means by which He often works. The apostles prepared, organized, and delegated, but they also remained open to the Spirit's redirection (Acts 16:6–10). As leaders, we must walk in that same tension: doing our part to be ready while trusting God to do His part in leading.[135] So the question remains: As a small group leader, how can I prepare with faith while remaining sensitive to the Spirit's leading?

Group Size, Length, and Frequency

The New Testament reminds us that God is a God of order, not of confusion (1 Corinthians 14:33). Structure in small groups is not meant to quench the Spirit but to create space for Him to move freely. From leading and managing groups myself, I have seen both the blessings of well-formed rhythms and the challenges when structure is missing. While circumstances such as limited leaders or available space may stretch groups beyond the ideal, best practices give us a framework to pursue faithfulness. And we must also remember that small groups are not confined to a church campus, homes, coffee shops, and even workplaces can become sacred spaces for discipleship. What matters is that believers are gathering to grow in Christ and encourage one another (Acts 2:46; Hebrews 10:24–25).

- **Size:** Aim for 8–12 people. This range invites participation without overwhelming the room or the leader (cf. 1 Corinthians 12:14–27 on every member's contribution).

---

[135] See Gladen, *Small Groups with Purpose*; Donahue, *Leading Life-Changing Small Groups*; Stanley and Willits, *Creating Community*; Braddy, "Six Keys to Organizing and Leading Sunday School Classes and Groups"; Comiskey, *How to Lead a Great Cell Group Meeting*.

- **Meeting length:** 60–90 minutes is typically ideal—long enough for fellowship, the Word, and prayer, while respecting schedules (Matthew 5:37; let your "yes" to the calendar be reliable).

- **Frequency:** Weekly gatherings build rhythm and trust (Hebrews 10:24–25). Twice a month can work, but momentum usually slows when meetings are irregular.

- **When to multiply:** If attendance consistently reaches 16–18, begin preparing an apprentice to launch a new group (not a reactive "split," but a sent team with blessing; Acts 13:2–3). This subject is explained in detail chapter 11.

Ultimately, numbers and logistics are tools, not the mission. A group of twelve may be healthy, and at times a group of twenty may still flourish, but the guiding principle is always spiritual growth and disciple-making. As Paul taught, the body works best when every member plays its part (1 Corinthians 12:14–27). These practices, thoughtful size, intentional length, consistent frequency, and Spirit-led multiplication, help us create spaces where discipleship thrives. Whether gathered in a living room, around a table at a coffee shop, or in a classroom on campus, the goal is the same: to build up one another in Christ and to carry His mission forward.[136]

---

[136] See Gladen, *Small Groups with Purpose*; Donahue, *Leading Life-Changing Small Groups*; Stanley and Willits, *Creating Community*; Braddy, "Six Keys to Organizing and Leading Sunday School Classes and Groups"; Comiskey, *How to Lead a Great Cell Group Meeting*.

Key Roles: Shared Ownership over Solo Leadership

Healthy groups distribute responsibility so that everyone grows and no one burns out (Ephesians 4:12; Romans 12:4–8). This area of structure is one where I personally need the most growth. Delegation has never come easily for me. It is not that I want to do everything myself, but I often hesitate to ask others to participate because I do not want to feel like I am burdening them. Whatever your reason may be, the truth is the same: leaders cannot function as a Lone Ranger and still have a healthy, successful group. Consider these roles in your small group organization:

- **Leader:** Shepherds the group spiritually, facilitates Scripture discussion, models disciple-making.

- **Apprentice Leader:** Learns alongside the leader with the goal of launching a new group within 6–12 months (2 Timothy 2:2).

- **Host / Fellowship Coordinator:** Curates the environment (room, seating, refreshments) and plans periodic socials (Acts 2:46–47).

- **Prayer & Care Coordinator:** Tracks requests, birthdays, needs, and follow-ups; mobilizes mid-week prayer (James 5:16; Galatians 6:2).

- **Outreach / Assimilation Leader:** Welcomes guests, follows up with newcomers and absentees within 24–48 hours (Romans 15:7).

- **Service / Missions Coordinator:** Connects the group to tangible service and witness (Micah 6:8; Matthew 5:16; Acts 1:8).

Provide one-paragraph role descriptions, each with 2–3 clear wins identified for every role. Make these descriptions available for the group and rotate tasks quarterly so more people can learn and lead. Using these guidelines is a great way to help individuals discover gifts and abilities they may not have realized they had.[137]

Apprentice Pathway: From Serving to Sending

Apprenticeship is more than shadowing; it is an intentional process of development. A simple pathway might look like this:

- **Serve:** Apprentice begins by taking small responsibilities (refreshments, reminders).

- **Lead a Segment:** Apprentice leads prayer, then discussion questions.

- **Lead the Group:** Apprentice plans and facilitates the whole gathering while the leader coaches.

- **Launch:** Apprentice is commissioned with a team to begin a new group.

---

[137] See Gladen, *Small Groups with Purpose*; Donahue, *Leading Life-Changing Small Groups*; Stanley and Willits, *Creating Community*; Braddy, "Six Keys to Organizing and Leading Sunday School Classes and Groups"; Comiskey, *How to Lead a Great Cell Group Meeting*.

This pathway reflects Paul's charge in 2 Timothy 2:2 and Jesus's Great Commission, that disciples who make disciples require intentional relationships and preparation (see Appendix 3).

(see Appendix 3)

Apprentice Pathway: From Serving to Sending

| Serve | Lead a Segment | Lead the Group | Launch |

A Reproducible Weekly Rhythm

Healthy groups grow when their rhythm is both simple and sustainable. The goal is not to create a rigid script but a reproducible pattern that any trained member could lead if needed. Structure should serve discipleship, not stifle it. Think of it as a trellis, not a cage—a framework that supports Spirit-led growth.[138]

A balanced weekly plan might look like this:

- **Welcome & Fellowship (10 min):** Begin with warm greetings and genuine connection. These few minutes set the tone of belonging and remind the group that discipleship happens in the context of love and family (Romans 12:10).

- **Prayer & Worship (10 min):** Lift hearts in gratitude and dependence on God. A song, a Psalm, or a prayer of thanks turns attention away from ourselves and toward the Lord (Psalm 100; Colossians 3:16).

---

[138] See Gladen, *Small Groups with Purpose*; Donahue, *Leading Life-Changing Small Groups*; Stanley and Willits, *Creating Community*; Braddy, "Six Keys to Organizing and Leading Sunday School Classes and Groups"; Comiskey, *How to Lead a Great Cell Group Meeting*.

- **Bible Study & Discussion (30–40 min):** Place God's Word at the center. Encourage interaction, observation, and application. Aim for discovery through Scripture rather than mere information transfer (Acts 2:42).

- **Application & Accountability (10–15 min):** Don't just ask, "What did we learn?" Ask, "What will we do?" Identify clear next steps and follow up weekly. Obedience, not just knowledge, marks discipleship (James 1:22; Hebrews 3:13).

- **Prayer for Needs & Mission (10 min):** Close by interceding for group members and for those far from Christ. Healthy groups pray both inwardly (for one another) and outwardly (for the lost and for God's mission) (James 5:16; 1 Timothy 2:1–4).

Communication Systems That Care for People

Healthy groups don't just connect when the chairs are set in a circle—they stay connected throughout the week. Shepherding requires both presence and intentional follow-up. Scripture reminds us, *"Know well the condition of your flocks, and give attention to your herds"* (Proverbs 27:23). In a small group, this means having simple, consistent systems of communication that ensure no one slips through the cracks. When messages are clear and care is intentional, people feel valued, prayed for, and drawn deeper into community.

- **Weekly Reminder:** Send a text or email 24–48 hours before the meeting with time, location, and Scripture.

- **Mid-Week Prayer Touch:** Share updated requests and answered prayers; invite one-sentence praise reports (Philippians 4:6–7).

- **Guest & Absentee Follow-Up:** Greet guests the same day and check on absentees within two days (Luke 15 heart for the one).

- **Shared Calendar / Thread:** Use one channel (text thread, email list, or app) to avoid message scatter.

Here is a cadence example of intentional communication:

- **Sun/Mon:** Thank-you + highlights
- **Wed:** Prayer updates
- **Fri/Sat:** Reminder + Scripture preview

Healthy communication builds belonging. When someone misses and no one reaches out, they may quietly conclude they are not truly missed. But when a guest receives a text the same evening, or an absent member gets a caring call, the message is clear: "You matter to this group." These small acts of follow-up are not just logistics; they are moments of shepherding. As Jesus taught in Luke 15, the shepherd leaves the ninety-nine to pursue the one; our communication rhythms echo that same heart.[139]

---

[139] See Gladen, *Small Groups with Purpose*; Donahue, *Leading Life-Changing Small Groups*; Stanley and Willits, *Creating Community*; Braddy, "Six Keys to Organizing and Leading Sunday School Classes and Groups"; Comiskey, *How to Lead a Great Cell Group Meeting*.

Planning for Multiplication (Before You "Need" It)

Multiplication is not a backup plan for discipleship but the very goal from the beginning. It requires intentional planning, not something tacked on at the end of the process. When leaders start with multiplication in mind, they set a trajectory for lasting impact and continual growth. This concept will be explored in greater detail in chapter 11, but it is important to start early by embedding multiplication into the very fabric of discipleship.

- **Identify an Apprentice (Month 1):** Share your heart and expectations; pray together (Luke 6:12–13).

- **Gradual Handoffs (Months 2–4):** Apprentice leads welcome, then prayer, then discussion, then the full meeting. Offer feedback after each step.

- **Co-Lead & Coach (Months 5–6):** Apprentice designs the plan; you shadow and coach.

- **Commission & Launch (Month 6+):** Celebrate, lay hands, and send with 2–3 others if possible (Acts 13:3).

Stewarding the Room: Environment that Serves the Mission

Some of these principles were introduced earlier when we discussed presentation (Chapter 5), but they bear repeating here with an emphasis on organization and stewardship. A group's physical environment shapes how people engage the Word and one another. Jesus Himself used intentional order when He had the crowds sit in groups before feeding them (Mark 6:39–40).

Thoughtful preparation of the room removes distractions and builds a setting where the Spirit's work is unhindered.[140]

- **Seating:** While we noted earlier that circles invite conversation, here the emphasis is stewardship. Leaders steward space to reinforce mission, circles encourage dialogue as equals under God's Word, while rows risk turning participants into passive listeners. Keep the arrangement simple, comfortable, and conducive to connection (Acts 2:42).

- **Time:** Time management is more than presentation; it is an organizational act of faithfulness. Beginning and ending when promised builds credibility. Jesus taught, *"Let your 'Yes' be yes"* (Matthew 5:37). A disciplined rhythm says to members, "Your time matters because your discipleship matters."

- **Accessibility:** Beyond presentation clarity, accessibility in organization removes unnecessary barriers to participation. Directions, signage, parking, and childcare provision declare in action, "You are welcome here." Jesus insisted, *"Let the children come to me; do not hinder them"* (Mark 10:14). Every logistical detail is an opportunity to extend Christ's welcome.

- **Hospitality:** In presentation, we touched on warmth; here, hospitality is seen as stewardship. Simple refreshments are not an afterthought but a tool that lowers defenses and fosters community. The Emmaus story reminds us that hearts often burn within us when

---

[140] See Gladen, *Small Groups with Purpose*; Donahue, *Leading Life-Changing Small Groups*; Stanley and Willits, *Creating Community*; Braddy, "Six Keys to Organizing and Leading Sunday School Classes and Groups"; Comiskey, *How to Lead a Great Cell Group Meeting*.

fellowship and Scripture meet around the table (Luke 24:30–32). The goal is not food itself but the deeper communion it can spark.

A well-prepared room communicates more than organization, it communicates expectation. It tells participants, "You were thought of before you arrived." That quiets anxieties for newcomers, signals value to regulars, and allows everyone to turn their attention more fully to Christ. In this way, even chairs, lighting, and refreshments become instruments of love when stewarded for the mission.[141] The diagram below illustrates an organized classroom layout.

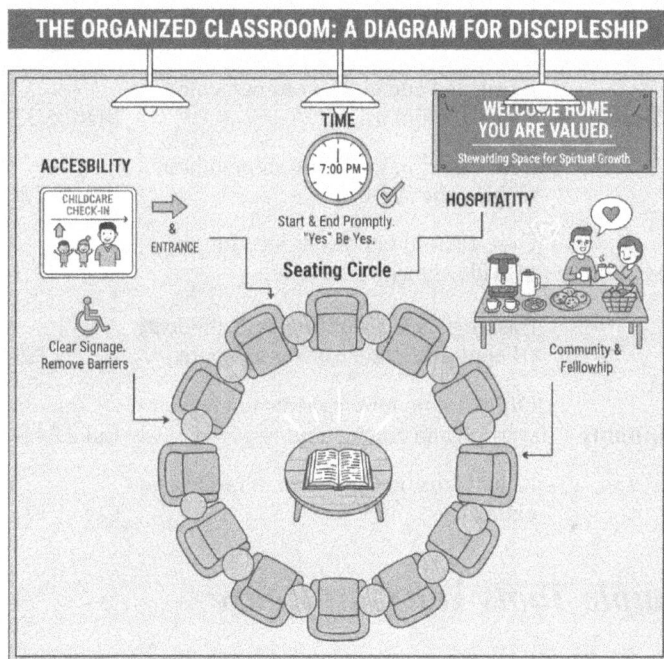

THE ORGANIZED CLASSROOM: A DIAGRAM FOR DISCIPLESHIP

TIME
7:00 PM

WELCOME HOME.
YOU ARE VALUED.
Stewarding Space for Spiritual Growth

ACCESBILITY

CHILDCARE CHECK-IN
& ENTRANCE

Start & End Promptly.
"Yes" Be Yes.

HOSPITATITY

Seating Circle

Clear Signage.
Remove Barriers

Community & Felllowhip

Thoughtful Preparation: Removing Distractions, Building Connection

141 See Gladen, *Small Groups with Purpose*; Donahue, *Leading Life-Changing Small Groups*; Stanley and Willits, *Creating Community*; Braddy, "Six Keys to Organizing and Leading Sunday School Classes and Groups"; Comiskey, *How to Lead a Great Cell Group Meeting*.

Room Readiness Checklist

This checklist helps small group leaders steward the environment so that the room serves the mission of making disciples. Each item is rooted in Scripture and designed to remove distractions while fostering fellowship, prayer, and the Word.

Category	Checklist Item	Scripture
Seating	Arrange chairs in a circle to encourage dialogue; avoid rows that create spectators.	Acts 2:42
	Provide enough chairs for comfort without overcrowding.	Mark 6:39-40
Time	Begin and end at the communicated times to build trust.	Matt. 5:37
	Leave margin for fellowship without rushing the Word.	Eph. 5:15-16
Accessibility	Give clear directions to location; provide signage if needed.	Mark 10:14
	Ensure parking, lighting, and childcare (if applicable) are easy to navigate.	Heb. 13:2
Hospitality	Offer simple refreshments to create warmth and connection.	Luke 24:30-32
	Keep focus on Christ, not on food or extras.	Col. 3:17

Simple Tools You Can Reuse

Healthy disciple-making groups don't need complex systems. Instead, they thrive when leaders are equipped with simple, repeatable tools that lighten the load and multiply effectiveness. Tools make that entrusting process tangible. By keeping resources simple, leaders free themselves from constant reinvention and give apprentices reproducible models they can carry forward.

- **One-Page Role Cards:** Every leader and helper benefits from clarity. A one-page card with the role title, 2–3 key responsibilities, and a few examples of "weekly wins" helps team members know what success looks like. These cards are easy to hand to an apprentice or rotate among group members, reinforcing shared ownership (Ephesians 4:12).

- **90-Day Launch Plan:** Multiplication requires planning, not guesswork. A simple three-month calendar that maps apprentice handoffs (when they lead prayer, facilitate discussion, or handle logistics) and a target launch date keeps everyone moving toward reproduction. This tool transforms vague hopes into actionable steps.

- **Attendance & Care Tracker:** Shepherding the flock means knowing who is present, who is missing, and how each member is doing spiritually (Proverbs 27:23). A weekly tracker gives space to record guests, note absences, log prayer requests, and mark follow-ups. Over time, this record becomes a visible testimony of God's faithfulness and the group's growth.

- **Meeting Planner:** Leaders don't need to script everything, but a simple planner keeps the meeting intentional. Include the passage to be studied, the desired outcome (what step of obedience you're praying for), discussion questions, time boxes for each section, and the name of who is leading each part. This keeps the group on mission and trains apprentices by giving them clear pieces to lead (see Appendix 5).

These tools don't replace the Holy Spirit's leading; they provide a trellis that supports growth. Their simplicity makes them easy to pass on, ensuring that discipleship is not only happening but multiplying.[142]

Small Group Leader Toolkit

Tool	Purpose	Key Elements	Scripture Anchor
One-Page Role Cards	Clarify responsibilities and define weekly "wins."	Role title—2-3 responsibilities —Weekly wins snapshot	Ephesians 4:12
90-Day Launch Plan	Create a timeline for apprentice development and group multiplication.	12-week calendar — Apprentice handoff dates — Target launch date	2 Timothy 2:2
Attendance & Care Tracker	Shepherd people faithfully by tracking presence, prayer, and follow-up.	Weekly attendance — Guest/absentee notes — Prayer + follow-up log	Proverbs 27:23
Meeting Planner	Keep gatherings intentional and reproducible.	Passage & main outcome— Key questions — Time boxes — Who leads	Acts 2:42

---

[142] See Gladen, *Small Groups with Purpose*; Donahue, *Leading Life-Changing Small Groups*; Stanley and Willits, *Creating Community*; Braddy, "Six Keys to Organizing and Leading Sunday School Classes and Groups"; Comiskey, *How to Lead a Great Cell Group Meeting*.

Conclusion

Organization is an act of love. It is not about control but about creating space where people can flourish in Christ. Clear pathways invite participation, intentional systems ensure that no one is overlooked, and thoughtful structure makes multiplication possible. In this way, organization serves discipleship, it equips every believer to grow into maturity and to help others do the same, *"speaking the truth in love...joined and held together...so that the body builds itself up in love"* (Ephesians 4:15–16).

To neglect organization is to risk neglecting people. To embrace it is to reflect the Good Shepherd, who knows His sheep by name and ensures none are forgotten (John 10:3). Leaders must see structure not as an obstacle but as a channel through which love and discipleship flow. Let us take up the call to organize with faith, knowing that in doing so we create environments where every believer can be equipped, every need can be noticed, and every disciple can grow into maturity in Christ.

Reflective Questions

1. Have I delegated key roles, or am I trying to carry the group alone?

2. Is our size healthy, and do I have a multiplication plan with an apprentice?

3. Does our weekly structure balance fellowship, Scripture, application, and mission?

4. Are our communication rhythms clear and consistent so no one slips through the cracks?

5. What two improvements will I implement in the next 30 days to strengthen organization for disciple-making?

Chapter 10: Pastoral Care

"Shepherd the flock of God that is among you, exercising oversight, not under compulsion, but willingly, as God would have you; not for shameful gain, but eagerly; not domineering over those in your charge, but being examples to the flock" — (1 Peter 5:2–3, ESV).

Why Pastoral Care?

Pastoral care is central to the life of a small group because it reflects the very heart of Christ, the Good Shepherd (John 10:11). Jesus modeled shepherding by knowing His sheep, calling them by name, protecting them from harm, and laying down His life for them. In the same way, small group leaders embody Christ's care for His people by praying for them, walking with them through hardship, and pointing them continually to the gospel.

Without pastoral care, groups risk becoming Bible studies without transformation or fellowships without depth. Paul reminded the Thessalonians that his ministry was marked by both tenderness and exhortation, *"We were gentle among you, like a nursing mother taking care of her own children…For you know how, like a father with his children, we exhorted each one of you and encouraged you and charged you to walk in a manner worthy of God"* (1 Thessalonians 2:7, 11–12, ESV). Shepherding keeps groups from drifting into programs and sustains them as spiritual families.

As Dietrich Bonhoeffer warned, "A Christian fellowship lives and exists by the intercession of its members for one another, or it collapses."[143] Pastoral care ensures that every believer is nurtured, supported, and anchored in Christ.[144]

Why Pastoral Care Matters for Discipleship

Discipleship is never only about information; it is about formation. Pastoral care ensures that truth is not only heard but lived. Jesus said, *"By this all people will know that you are my disciples, if you have love for one another"* (John 13:35). Care is the visible proof of discipleship. Without it, small groups risk becoming lecture halls instead of spiritual families.

Paul urged believers to *"bear one another's burdens, and so fulfill the law of Christ"* (Galatians 6:2). Discipleship without care ignores the law of Christ, which is love expressed in tangible action. When groups weave pastoral care into their rhythms, members see that following Christ is not merely an individual journey but a shared pilgrimage. In this way, pastoral care is discipleship in action. It grounds teaching in

---

[143] Dietrich Bonhoeffer, Life Together, 86.

[144] See Eugene H. Peterson, *The Contemplative Pastor: Returning to the Art of Spiritual Direction* (Grand Rapids: Eerdmans, 1989); Gregory C. Keck, *Counseling and Pastoral Care* (Nashville: Abingdon, 2002); Larry Crabb, *Connecting: Healing Ourselves and Our Relationships* (Nashville: Thomas Nelson, 1997); Ken Braddy, "Pastoral Care in Small Groups," Ken Braddy Blog, Lifeway, accessed September 27, 2025, https://kenbraddy.com; John MacArthur, *Pastoral Ministry: How to Shepherd Biblically* (Nashville: Thomas Nelson, 2005); Andrew Purves, *Pastoral Theology in the Classical Tradition* (Louisville: Westminster John Knox, 2001); Thomas C. Oden, *Pastoral Theology: Essentials of Ministry* (New York: HarperCollins, 1983).

love, transforms doctrine into devotion, and displays the heart of Christ to a watching world.[145]

The Shepherding Role of the Small Group Leader

Small group leaders are not merely facilitators of discussion but shepherds of people. In the ancient Middle Eastern culture of 2,000 years ago, shepherds carried a sacred responsibility for their flocks. Their daily work was not glamorous but demanding: they were to feed the flock, guide the flock, and protect the flock. Sheep were entirely dependent on their shepherd for provision, direction, and safety.

- **To Feed the Flock:** Shepherds led their sheep to pastures and water (Psalm 23:1–2). Without this, the sheep would starve or wander. Likewise, leaders must faithfully feed their groups with the Word of God, not with mere opinions (James 1:19-20).

- **To Lead the Flock:** Shepherds carried a staff to lead and redirect the sheep, ensuring they stayed on safe paths (Psalm 23:3). In the same way, leaders guide believers into obedience and maturity in Christ (Hebrews 13:17).

- **To Defend the Flock:** Shepherds defended their sheep from wolves, thieves, and other dangers (John 10:12–13). Small group leaders, as under-shepherds of Christ, protect their members from spiritual error and encourage them to remain steadfast in the truth (Acts 20:28–29).

---

[145] See Bonhoeffer, *Life Together*, 86; Peterson, *Contemplative Pastor*; Braddy, "Pastoral Care in Small Groups."

This imagery was so powerful that God often described His leaders as shepherds. The Lord told Ezekiel to confront false leaders who failed in their shepherding role, *"You eat the fat, you clothe yourselves with the wool…but you do not feed the sheep"* (Ezekiel 34:3). In contrast, Jesus declared, *"I am the good shepherd. The good shepherd lays down his life for the sheep"* (John 10:11).

The same expectations now rest on small group leaders. They are entrusted with the responsibility to know, feed, guide, and protect their members as under-shepherds of Christ. This calling demands a life of prayer, attentiveness, and sacrificial love.

Shepherding is not optional, it is woven into the biblical vision for leadership. As Paul taught, leaders are to *"equip the saints for the work of ministry, for building up the body of Christ"* (Ephesians 4:12). Pastoral care ensures that teaching and discipleship do not remain abstract but touch the real joys, struggles, and vulnerabilities of life.[146]

Knowing the Flock

Shepherds in the ancient world were not distant overseers; they knew their sheep. Jesus said, *"The sheep hear his voice, and he calls his own sheep by name and leads them out"* (John

---

[146] See Bonhoeffer, *Life Together*, 86; Peterson, *Contemplative Pastor*; Braddy, "Pastoral Care in Small Groups," MacArthur, *Pastoral Ministry,* Purves, *Pastoral Theology in the Classical Tradition,* Oden, *Pastoral Theology: Essentials of Ministry.*

10:3). Knowing the flock meant understanding their tendencies, weaknesses, and needs.

For small group leaders, knowing the flock means more than recognizing faces at a meeting. It means learning their stories, remembering their struggles, and rejoicing in their victories. Pastoral care begins with personal knowledge: names prayed over, burdens carried, lives remembered.

To shepherd well is to know the flock well. Without knowledge, feeding becomes generic, guidance misdirected, and protection unfocused. Leaders who know their people by name mirror the Good Shepherd who knows His own and is known by them (John 10:14).[147]

The Limits of the Shepherd

Small group leaders must remember that they are under-shepherds, not saviors. Christ alone carries the full weight of His people's needs. Psalm 127:1 reminds us, *"Unless the Lord builds the house, those who build it labor in vain."* Our calling is faithful obedience, not ultimate results.

Jesus declared, *"Apart from me you can do nothing"* (John 15:5). Leaders who confuse their role with Christ's risk burnout and disappointment. True pastoral care points members not to the leader's strength but to the Chief Shepherd's sufficiency (1 Peter 5:4).

---

[147] See Bonhoeffer, *Life Together*, 86; Peterson, *Contemplative Pastor*; Braddy, "Pastoral Care in Small Groups," MacArthur, *Pastoral Ministry,* Purves, *Pastoral Theology in the Classical Tradition,* Oden, *Pastoral Theology: Essentials of Ministry.*

Healthy leaders accept their limits, rest in Christ, and remember that every act of care is a signpost pointing to the One who never leaves nor forsakes His flock.[148]

Caring Through Prayer, Encouragement, and Presence

- **Prayer is the first act of care.** Leaders should regularly intercede for members by name, keeping a record of requests and answers to encourage faith. J. C. Ryle wrote, "Prayer is the very life-breath of true Christianity."[149]

- **Encouragement is also vital.** Paul commanded, *"Encourage one another and build one another up"* (1 Thessalonians 5:11). A quick text, a handwritten card, or a phone call can remind someone that they are loved and not forgotten.

- **Presence matters most.** Leaders shepherd not from a distance but through proximity—celebrating milestones, sitting with grieving families, visiting the sick, and simply showing up. This incarnational presence mirrors Christ, who dwelt among His people (John 1:14).

---

[148] See Bonhoeffer, *Life Together*, 86; Peterson, *Contemplative Pastor*; Braddy, "Pastoral Care in Small Groups," MacArthur, *Pastoral Ministry,* Purves, *Pastoral Theology in the Classical Tradition,* Oden, *Pastoral Theology: Essentials of Ministry.*

[149] J. C. Ryle, A Call to Prayer (London: William Hunt, 1877), 8.

Practices of Pastoral Care

Pastoral care is expressed through consistent, intentional practices: Healthy small groups are not built on teaching alone; they are sustained by love expressed through consistent, intentional care. Paul reminded the Thessalonians, *"We were ready to share with you not only the gospel of God but also our own selves"* (1 Thessalonians 2:8). This is the essence of pastoral care within a group, truth shared in the context of genuine presence.[150] Pastoral care comes in two expressions:

- **Reactive Care responds to the immediate needs of life,** for example, grief, crisis, illness, and loss. This reflects Paul's call to *"comfort those who are in any affliction"* with the same comfort we receive from God (2 Corinthians 1:4).

- **Proactive Care creates rhythms of health before crises arrive.** This will look like, regular check-ins, prayer partnerships, accountability questions, encouragement, and celebration of milestones. This reflects the call to *"consider how to stir up one another to love and good works"* (Hebrews 10:24).

Healthy groups need both. **Reactive care** ensures no one walks alone in hardship; **proactive care** strengthens discipleship so that faith is resilient when storms come. When these practices are woven into the life of a small group, pastoral care becomes a shared culture rather than a burden carried by the leader alone. Members experience the love of

---

[150] See Bonhoeffer, *Life Together*, 86; Peterson, *Contemplative Pastor*; Braddy, "Pastoral Care in Small Groups," MacArthur, *Pastoral Ministry*, Purves, *Pastoral Theology in the Classical Tradition*, Oden, *Pastoral Theology: Essentials of Ministry*.

Christ through one another, and the group becomes more than a meeting; it becomes a spiritual family, marked by the kind of love Jesus said would show the world we are His disciples (John 13:35).

Caring for Different Needs

Every small group carries a diversity of needs, because every believer is walking through different seasons of life. Pastoral care within a group means noticing these needs and responding with the love of Christ. Healthy groups do not try to meet every need perfectly, but they become the first line of support within the church, walking together in ways that point back to Christ as the ultimate Shepherd.

- **Spiritual Needs:** Growth in Discipleship (2 Timothy 3:16–17). The deepest need of every believer is to grow in Christlikeness. Scripture teaches, reproves, corrects, and trains us so that we are *"equipped for every good work."* Healthy groups prioritize discipleship through God's Word, prayer, repentance, and mutual encouragement. Pastoral care means ensuring that spiritual growth is not neglected in the midst of other needs.

- **Emotional Needs:** Comfort in Struggles (2 Corinthians 1:3–4). Paul reminds us that God is the *"Father of mercies and God of all comfort, who comforts us in all our affliction, so that we may be able to comfort those who are in any affliction."* Healthy groups embody this by being present in grief, listening during seasons of stress, and providing a safe place to be honest. Emotional care does not replace professional help when needed, but it does provide a faithful community where burdens are shared and hearts are encouraged.

- **Physical Needs:** Tangible Acts of Love (Acts 2:44–45). The early church *"had all things in common"* and shared as anyone had need. Healthy groups reflect this same spirit of generosity and care: providing meals in times of illness, helping with transportation, stepping in with financial assistance when appropriate, or serving through practical projects. Meeting physical needs shows the gospel in action and displays Christ's love in tangible ways.

- **Missional Needs:** Serving and Witnessing Together (Matthew 28:19–20). Groups are not only inwardly focused but outwardly sent. Jesus commanded His followers to make disciples of all nations, and small groups are one of the best launching points for mission. Whether serving in the community, supporting a missionary, or practicing evangelism through shared outreach, healthy groups care for one another by pushing each other toward gospel mission.

When small groups recognize and respond to these dimensions of care, spiritual, emotional, physical, and missional, they reflect the wholeness of Christ's ministry. Jesus taught, comforted, healed, and sent His disciples on mission. A healthy group that cares across these four areas becomes a spiritual family where needs are not ignored, Christ's presence is made tangible, and the love of God overflows to others.[151]

---

[151] See Bonhoeffer, *Life Together*, 86; Peterson, *Contemplative Pastor*; Braddy, "Pastoral Care in Small Groups," MacArthur, *Pastoral Ministry*, Purves, *Pastoral Theology in the Classical Tradition*, Oden, *Pastoral Theology: Essentials of Ministry.*

The Cost and Reward of Shepherding

Pastoral care often comes with a cost. Paul expressed it this way, *"I will most gladly spend and be spent for your souls"* (2 Corinthians 12:15). Shepherding requires emotional energy, time, and sacrifice. Leaders may feel stretched, unseen, or even drained in the work of care.

Yet the reward is eternal. God promises that *"He is not unjust so as to overlook your work and the love that you have shown for His name in serving the saints"* (Hebrews 6:10). Peter assures leaders that *"when the Chief Shepherd appears, you will receive the unfading crown of glory"* (1 Peter 5:4). The cost is real, but the reward is greater. Every act of care sows eternal fruit in the lives of believers and brings joy to the heart of God.[152]

Handling Crises and Setting Boundaries

Life inevitably brings crises—illness, broken relationships, financial struggles, and the death of loved ones. As a pastor and group leader, I have walked with people through many of these moments. Each situation is unique, and often one of the best ways to care is not through polished words but through presence. Sometimes the ministry of presence, sitting, listening, even weeping in silence is the most Christlike response. A small group can be a lifeline of love, prayer, and support in such times. The worst thing leaders can do is ignore or minimize a crisis; people must feel seen, connected, and supported.

---

[152] See Bonhoeffer, *Life Together*, 86; Peterson, *Contemplative Pastor*; Braddy, "Pastoral Care in Small Groups."

At the same time, leaders must practice wisdom in setting boundaries. Paul provides a helpful balance when he says, *"Bear one another's burdens"* (Galatians 6:2), but also, *"each will have to bear his own load"* (Galatians 6:5). Both are true: we walk with others, but we do not carry responsibility for their lives. Some situations, such as abuse, severe depression, or complex family crises, require referral to pastors, counselors, or professionals. Leaders serve best not as saviors but as shepherds under Christ, pointing people to the Lord who is their ultimate refuge, *"God is our refuge and strength, a very present help in trouble"* (Psalm 46:1)
.

Boundaries protect both the leader and the group. As Peter Scazzero notes, "We cannot give what we do not possess."[153] Leaders must guard their emotional, physical, and spiritual health, remembering that they are shepherds, not saviors. Emotional, physical, and spiritual health must be guarded if leaders are to serve others well. Sabbath rest, self-care, and prayer are not indulgences but acts of obedience. Jesus Himself invites the weary, *"Come to me, all who labor and are heavy laden, and I will give you rest"* (Matthew 11:28). Saying "no" to some demands is often saying "yes" to God's best (Matthew 5:37).[154]

Healthy boundaries also model maturity for the group. Leaders who are resilient demonstrate that strength comes not from constant activity but from abiding in Christ. As Nehemiah declared, *"The joy of the Lord is your strength"* (Nehemiah

---

[153] Peter Scazzero, The Emotionally Healthy Leader: How Transforming Your Inner Life Will Deeply Transform Your Church, Team, and the World (Grand Rapids: Zondervan, 2015), 23.

[154] Peter Scazzero, Emotionally Healthy Spirituality: It's Impossible to Be Spiritually Mature, While Remaining Emotionally Immature (Nashville: Thomas Nelson, 2017), 72.

8:10). By practicing rest, self-awareness, and wise delegation, leaders embody the truth that we are finite, dependent creatures sustained by God's presence and grace. As David Murray observes, "To be resilient, we must learn to stop and rest as God designed."[155]

Handling crises faithfully means leaning into compassion without falling into codependency, and setting boundaries means embracing God's design for sustainable ministry. Together, these practices equip leaders to walk alongside others with empathy, while keeping Christ at the center of care.[156] Please review the six steps of *Crisis Care Pathway for Small Group Leaders* on the next page.

CRISIS CARE PATHWAY

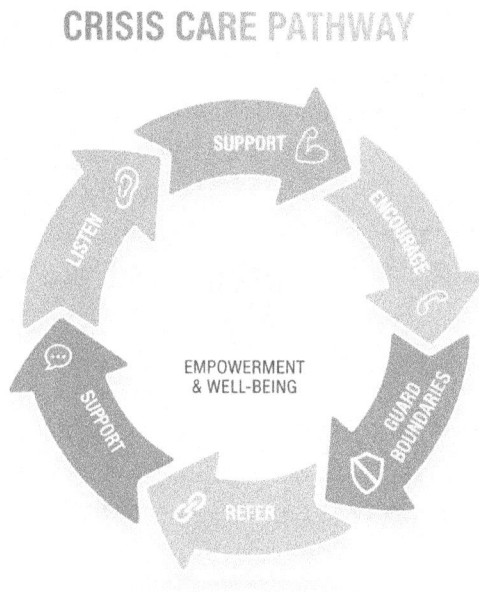

SUPPORT

ENCOURAGE

LISTEN

EMPOWERMENT & WELL-BEING

SUPPORT

GUARD BOUNDARIES

REFER

---

[155] David Murray and Tom Karel, *A Christian's Guide to Mental Illness: Answers to 30 Common Questions* (Wheaton, IL: Crossway, 2021), 114.

[156] See Bonhoeffer, *Life Together*, 86; Peterson, *Contemplative Pastor*; Braddy, "Pastoral Care in Small Groups."

Crisis Care Pathway for Small Group Leaders

Step	Biblical Foundation	Practical Advice	Key Action
1. Listen with Compassion	Jas. 1:19	Presence matters more than quick solutions. Avoid clichés; listen with empathy.	Offer a listening ear before giving advice.
2. Support through Prayer & Presence	Ga.l 6:2	Pray immediately. Presence through meals, texts, and silence can be ministry.	Be there with tangible love.
3. Encourage Hope in God	Ps. 46:1	Share God's promises without minimizing pain. Use Scripture for comfort (Ps. 34:18; Matt. 11:28-30; Rom. 8:38-39).	Point them to God's faithfulness.
4. Refer When Needed	Gal. 6:5	Know your limits. Some crises need pastoral or professional care. Referring is wise stewardship.	Keep a referral list ready.
5. Follow Up with Care	1 Thess. 2:8	Check in with calls, texts, or visits. Show they are not forgotten after the crisis moment.	Consistent follow-up communicates love.
6. Guard Boundaries & Practice Self-Care	Luke 5:16	You are a shepherd, not the Savior. Rest and saying "no" are necessary.	Balance compassion with limits. Healthy leaders lead healthy groups.

Using the Church Body in Crises

Leaders must also remember that they are not meant to carry crises alone. God designed the church as a body where care is shared. In Acts 6, when the daily distribution to widows was neglected, the apostles appointed servants to ensure no one was overlooked. This reminds us that care is a ministry of the whole church, not the burden of one leader.

When crises arise, leaders should partner with pastors, deacons, and other ministries. This not only provides greater support but also models the truth that we are one body, many members, serving one another in love (1 Corinthians 12:12–27).

Equipping the Group to Shepherd One Another

The goal of pastoral care is not to create dependency on one leader, but to equip the group to care for one another. Paul reminds us that leaders exist *"to equip the saints for the work of ministry"* (Ephesians 4:12). This means that the role of a leader is not to carry every burden personally but to train and encourage the group to share in caring for one another.

Leaders can put this into practice in several simple but powerful ways. They can pair members together as prayer partners, ensuring that everyone is both praying for and being prayed for. They can rotate responsibilities for meals, follow-ups, or words of encouragement, giving different members the opportunity to serve. Finally, they can encourage each member to commit to one intentional act of care per week, whether sending a text, offering a prayer, or making a visit. These small steps create a culture of mutual care, reminding the group that every member has a part to play in building up the body of Christ. When every member participates, the group matures into a true family. Care is multiplied, leaders are sustained, and the love of Christ flows freely through the body.[157]

Building a Culture of Mutual Care

The healthiest groups do not orbit around a single leader, they become families where the whole body ministers to one another. Paul wrote, *"that there may be no division in the body, but that the members may have the same care for one another"* (1 Corinthians 12:25). Leaders model this by humbly sharing their own needs, inviting prayer, and equipping members to serve each other. Over time, care becomes natural: members check in, meals appear at doorsteps, texts of encouragement are sent, and no one walks alone. Mutual care is not a program; it is the evidence of Holy Spirit-filled life together.

Practical Tools for Cultivating Mutual Care

- **Prayer Lists:** Sharing the Burdens (Galatians 6:2). Keep a running, updated list of needs. Pray over them in meetings, but also encourage members to pray during the week. Rotate who leads prayer so the responsibility is shared.

- **Care Teams:** Everyone Engaged (Philippians 2:4). Assign two or three members to check in on absentees or needs each week. This spreads responsibility and ensures no one slips through unnoticed.

---

[157] See Bonhoeffer, *Life Together*, 86; Peterson, *Contemplative Pastor*; Braddy, "Pastoral Care in Small Groups," MacArthur, *Pastoral Ministry,* Purves, *Pastoral Theology in the Classical Tradition,* Oden, *Pastoral Theology: Essentials of Ministry.*

- **Meal Trains / Service Rotations:** Love in Action (James 2:15–16). When someone faces illness, surgery, or loss, organize meals, childcare, or practical help. A shared spreadsheet or app can make sign-ups easy. Small acts of service preach the gospel louder than words.

- **Celebrations:** Marking God's Goodness (Romans 12:15). Acknowledge birthdays, anniversaries, new jobs, baptisms, and spiritual milestones. "Rejoice with those who rejoice, weep with those who weep." Celebrating both the highs and the lows reminds the group that every season matters to God.

- **Communication Channels:** Staying Connected (Hebrews 10:24–25). Use a group text, app, or email chain to keep encouragement flowing during the week. Share Scriptures, prayer requests, and updates. This keeps the fellowship alive beyond the meeting.[158]

The Fruit of Mutual Care

When these rhythms take root, groups become more than Bible studies—they become spiritual families. Needs are met, encouragement flows freely, and Christ is displayed in tangible love. Jesus said, *"By this all people will know that you are my disciples, if you have love for one another"* (John 13:35). Such practices foster what Bonhoeffer described as life together—a fellowship grounded in Christ and expressed through sacrificial love.[159]

---

[158] See Bonhoeffer, *Life Together*, 86; Peterson, *Contemplative Pastor*; Braddy, "Pastoral Care in Small Groups," MacArthur, *Pastoral Ministry,* Purves, *Pastoral Theology in the Classical Tradition,* Oden, *Pastoral Theology: Essentials of Ministry.*

[159] Dietrich Bonhoeffer, Life Together, 19.

Conclusion

Pastoral care is not an accessory to small group life, it is its heartbeat. It transforms groups from weekly meetings into spiritual families. Care ensures that truth is embodied, love is practiced, and discipleship is lived out in community.

Ultimately, pastoral care points beyond human leaders to Christ, the *"great shepherd of the sheep"* (Hebrews 13:20). He is the source of comfort, strength, and transformation. Leaders shepherd faithfully not to draw people to themselves but to point them to Him.

When groups embody pastoral care, they become living testimonies of the gospel. Needs are met, burdens are lifted, faith is strengthened, and Christ is glorified. Such communities declare to a watching world that Jesus is alive among His people.

Reflective Questions

1. Do I know the spiritual, emotional, and physical needs of my members?

2. Is prayer at the center of how I care for my group?

3. Am I equipping members to share in care, or am I carrying the load alone?

4. Do I have healthy boundaries that point people to Christ, not to myself?

5. Am I practicing resilience and rest so I can shepherd others well (cf. Matthew 11:28)?

Chapter 11: Multiplication

"What you have heard from me in the presence of many witnesses entrust to faithful men, who will be able to teach others also." — (2 Timothy 2:2, ESV)

Why Multiplication Matters

Multiplication is not a growth strategy; it is the New Testament pattern for gospel advance. Jesus formed and sent (Luke 6:12–13; Mark 6:7; Luke 10:1). The church in Acts prayed, commissioned, and planted (Acts 13:2–3; 14:23). Paul trained Timothy to train others, and he encouraged Titus to have older believers invest in younger believers (Titus 2). When groups only gather, they eventually stall; when they gather and reproduce, disciples, leaders, and new groups flourish for the good of the church and the mission of God (Matthew 28:18–20; Ephesians 4:11–16).

A Biblical Theology of Multiplication

A biblical theology of multiplication traces God's design for growth and sending from Genesis to the early church and beyond. From the very beginning, God's blessing aimed outward: humanity was commissioned to *"be fruitful and multiply"* (Genesis 1:28), and Abraham was called so that *"all the families of the earth"* would be blessed through him (Genesis 12:1–3). This trajectory of creation and covenant establishes that God's people are not meant to remain static but to expand, filling the earth with His glory.

Jesus embodied this same pattern in His ministry. He deliberately chose twelve men, forming them into a community (formation, Mark 3:13–15). He spent time with them, shaping their character and deepening their faith (development), and then sent them out to proclaim the good news and practice the works of the kingdom (deployment, Mark 6:7). Multiplication was never accidental in the life of Jesus; it was intentional, relational, and reproducible.

The apostles continued this pattern after Christ's ascension. The early church commissioned teams to carry the gospel to unreached places (Acts 13:2–3) and appointed leaders in every city where the gospel took root (Acts 14:23; Titus 1:5). Multiplication was not simply about adding converts but about establishing new communities of faith with mature leaders capable of shepherding others.

Paul articulated perhaps the clearest vision of multiplication when he urged Timothy to entrust what he had learned to *"faithful people who will be able to teach others also"* (2 Timothy 2:2). This four-generation model, Paul to Timothy, Timothy to faithful people, and those people to others, shows the long view of discipleship, ensuring the gospel advances beyond one generation of leaders.

Finally, the New Testament emphasizes that multiplication is not only the work of apostles or pastors but of the whole body. Every member is gifted by God for the building up of the church (Romans 12:4–8; 1 Corinthians 12). As believers speak the truth in love, the body grows and matures into Christ, who is the Head (Ephesians 4:12–16). Multiplication happens when the entire church participates in the mission, each part doing its work.

In summary, multiplication is the intentional formation and sending of disciples, the development and release of new leaders, and the planting of new groups that reproduce the same process. It is not merely a strategy but a biblical mandate, woven into creation, covenant, Christ, the apostles, and the body of Christ itself.[160]

The Apprenticeship Model

Healthy groups never leave leadership to chance. Instead, they cultivate a clear, relational pathway for raising up new leaders who will shepherd people and multiply ministry. One of the most helpful tools I use to identify potential leaders is the **CORE Framework,** looking for those who are **Character-**driven, **Obedient** to God, **Reliable** in their commitments, and **Equippable** for future growth. The following paragraphs break down each of these components in detail.

✿CORE Framework✿

LOOKING FOR THOSE WHO ARE:

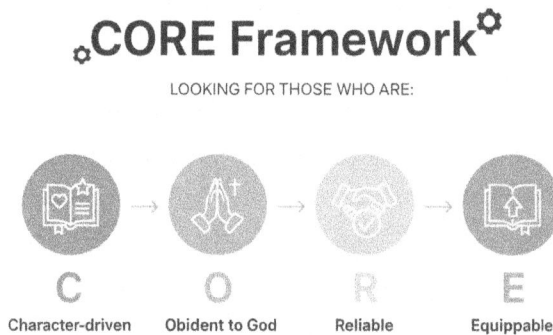

C	O	R	E
Character-driven	Obident to God	Reliable	Equippable

---

[160] See Steve Smith with Ying Kai, *T4T: A Discipleship Re-Revolution* (Monument, CO: WIGTake Resources, 2011); Dave Ferguson and Warren Bird, *Hero Maker: Five Essential Practices for Leaders to Multiply Leaders* (Grand Rapids: Zondervan, 2018); Ralph Moore, *Making Disciples: Developing Lifelong Followers of Jesus* (Grand Rapids: Baker Books, 2001); Jim Putman, Bobby Harrington, and Robert E. Coleman, *DiscipleShift: Five Steps That Help Your Church Make Disciples Who Make Disciples* (Grand Rapids: Zondervan, 2013); Mike Breen and Steve Cockram, *Building a Discipling Culture: How to Release a Missional Movement by Discipling People Like Jesus Did* (Pawleys Island, SC: 3DM Publishing, 2011); Ken Braddy, "Why Multiplication Matters in Groups," Ken Braddy Blog, Lifeway, accessed September 27, 2025, https://kenbraddy.com.

- **Character (Titus 1:7–9):** Paul's profile for spiritual leaders emphasizes a settled life shaped by the gospel: above reproach, self-controlled, hospitable, disciplined, holding to sound doctrine. For an apprentice, you are not demanding elder-level maturity, but you are looking for trajectory: a person increasingly governed by Scripture, repentant when wrong, gracious under pressure, and safe with people.

    - **Observable marks:** They speak truth without harshness; guards confidences; practices hospitality; receives correction without defensiveness (Proverbs 12:1; 27:6).

    - **Red flags:** They are chronic sarcasm, unresolved conflict, gossip, volatility, or a pattern of unkept commitments.

- **Obedient (John 14:23):** *"If anyone loves me, he will keep my word."* Apprenticeship is not primarily a skill course; it is a love-for-Christ course that shows up in practical obedience. Look for doers of the word (James 1:22); someone who applies Scripture between meetings, reconciles quickly (Matthew 5:23–24), and aligns with church leadership and doctrine (Hebrews 13:17).

    - **Observable marks:** They are quick to repent; initiates peacemaking; practices the basics, Word, prayer, witness, generosity.

    - **Red flags:** They have selective obedience, persistent excuse-making, or resistance to biblical counsel.

- **Reliable (Luke 16:10):** *"One who is faithful in a very little is also faithful in much."* Before you hand someone a group, hand them small stewardship and watch for follow-through. Reliability is love expressed in showing up, showing care, and seeing it through.

- **Observable marks:** They are on time, prepared, responsive; follows up with newcomers; closes loops without reminders.

- **Micro-tests:** They send the agenda to three people by Thursday; confirm a meal train; text three prayer check-ins, then review.

- **Equippable (Ephesians 4:12);** Christ gives leaders *"to equip the saints for the work of ministry."* An equippable person is coachable—hungry to learn, eager to practice, and humble enough to be corrected, and has the intent to equip others. You're not just training a helper; you're shaping a future multiplier.

  - **Observable marks:** takes notes, asks clarifying questions, tries new skills, invites feedback, and can teach back what they learned (Proverbs 9:9; Philippians 4:9).

  - **Simple test:** "Could you show a new believer how to pray 10 minutes a day and then ask them to show someone else?"[161]

How to Develop: A Four-Step Progression

Developing new leaders in small groups follows a four-step progression that blends biblical principles with practical

---

[161] See Smith and Kai, *T4T*; Ferguson and Bird, *Hero Maker*; Braddy, "Why Multiplication Matters in Groups."

checkpoints. The first step is **Observe** (Philippians 4:9), where the leader models a rhythm of welcome, Word, prayer, care, and mission while the apprentice watches for both structure and tone. Within two to three weeks, the apprentice should be able to describe the meeting flow and identify ways the leader draws quieter members into participation.

The second step is **Assist**, which involves giving the apprentice real ownership by assigning tangible tasks such as opening or closing in prayer, managing attendance and follow-up, organizing a meal, or sharing a short Scripture. By four to six weeks, the apprentice should reliably handle at least two roles and initiate care without prompting.

The third step is **Lead with Coaching** (Acts 18:26). At this stage, the apprentice facilitates discussion while the leader observes, later debriefing privately with two questions: "What fed the group?" and "What would you tighten?" By six to ten weeks, the apprentice should be able to craft five to seven open-ended questions from the passage, lead prayer beyond requests (Colossians 4:2–4), and redirect the group graciously.

The final step is **Launch & Support** (Acts 13:2–3), where the apprentice is commissioned to begin a new group or transition into leading the current one. In the first six to eight weeks post-launch, the leader provides coaching touchpoints and checks on the group's health in areas such as attendance, care rhythms, and identification of future apprentices. This process ensures multiplication of healthy groups through intentional mentoring, biblical accountability, and practical leadership development.[162]

---

[162] See Smith and Kai, *T4T*; Ferguson and Bird, *Hero Maker*; Braddy, "Why Multiplication Matters in Groups."

Meet Monthly One-on-One (Proverbs 27:17)

A healthy rhythm for developing apprentices and small group leaders is to meet monthly one-on-one (Proverbs 27:17) for about 30–45 minutes with a clear, intentional agenda. Begin with **Word and Prayer** (10 minutes), reading and praying through a leader-forming passage such as 2 Timothy 2:1–2 or 1 Peter 5:2–3 to ground the meeting in Scripture. Move into a **Debrief** (10 minutes), asking what went well in the past month and where tension appeared, whether in time management, dominant talkers, or moments requiring tenderness.

Next, give attention to a **Skill Focus** (10 minutes), developing one micro-skill such as asking good follow-up questions, closing discussions effectively, or guiding prayer that flows from Scripture. Follow this with **Plan and People** (5 minutes), identifying who needs shepherding in the coming week and clarifying one practical step of care or discipleship.

Conclude with setting **Targets** (2 minutes), choosing two small, specific, and dated goals, for example, "Draft next week's 5–7 discussion questions by Wednesday 8pm" or "Coach Sam to share his three-minute testimony this Wednesday at 6pm." Throughout, adopt a **Coaching Posture** of encouragement first by naming evidences of grace, then offering one clear improvement, and finishing with prayer. Keeping notes allows you to track growth and celebrate progress the following month.

Finally, establish a **Guardrail**, multiply groups for the sake of mission, not as a reaction to unresolved conflict or issues in the group (Romans 12:18; Ephesians 4:1–3). This structure ensures that one-on-one meetings remain focused, biblical, and catalytic for healthy leadership multiplication.[163]

Pathways for Multiplying Groups

Multiplication does not happen by accident—it happens through intentional pathways that reflect both biblical models and practical strategy. Acts 1:8 reminds us that the gospel is designed to expand outward, starting with a small circle and rippling into new communities. Healthy small groups embrace this same multiplying DNA.[164]

1. New Group Plant: An apprentice leader is intentionally trained and then launched with 4–6 volunteers from the sending group. This mirrors Paul's missionary journeys where he would appoint leaders and leave them to establish local gatherings (Acts 14:23). Sending a core allows the new group to start with relational strength and momentum.

2. Sub-Group to Group: Sometimes multiplication begins by dividing. Groups can break into gendered triads or quads for 8–12 weeks of focused discipleship (Proverbs 27:17). These sub-groups allow deeper accountability and practice of leadership. Over time, at least one of these triads matures into a new group with its own shepherding leader.

3. Missional Plant: Not all multiplication happens inside church walls. New groups can be started in places where people live, work, and gather—an apartment complex, a college campus, a military base, or among shift workers who

---

[163] Smith and Kai, *T4T*; Ferguson and Bird, *Hero Maker*; Braddy, "Why Multiplication Matters in Groups."

[164] Smith and Kai, *T4T*; Ferguson and Bird, *Hero Maker*; Braddy, "Why Multiplication Matters in Groups."

need flexible times. This follows the missional heartbeat of the early church; *"Every day, in the temple and from house to house, they did not cease teaching and preaching Jesus as the Christ"* (Acts 5:42).

4. Seasonal Accelerators: Short-term, 6–8 week "on-ramps" can serve as catalytic gatherings around a theme or book of the Bible. At the end, participants are encouraged to form multiple ongoing groups. This pattern reflects the way Jesus often gathered people for seasons of teaching (Matthew 5–7) before sending them to live it out in community.

Sending Well

Multiplication is not just a programmatic move; it is a spiritual act. Leaders and members being sent should be bathed in prayer, affirmed by their group, and publicly commissioned. The church at Antioch modeled this: *"While they were worshiping the Lord and fasting, the Holy Spirit said, 'Set apart for me Barnabas and Saul for the work to which I have called them.' Then after fasting and praying they laid their hands on them and sent them off"* (Acts 13:2–3).[165] The following are practical steps for sending well:

- Pray intentionally over new leaders and groups, asking God to grant boldness and endurance (Ephesians 6:18–20).

- Commission publicly so that multiplication is celebrated, not hidden.

---

[165] Smith and Kai, *T4T*; Ferguson and Bird, *Hero Maker*; Braddy, "Why Multiplication Matters in Groups."

- Mark milestones with 30- and 60-day check-ins for encouragement, coaching, and problem-solving.

- Celebrate stories of what God is doing, reinforcing a culture where sending is normal, not exceptional.

Multiplication is not loss, it is legacy. Every sending moment is a reminder that the Kingdom grows when God's people step out in faith, empowered by His Spirit, to make disciples who make disciples.

Barriers to Multiplication (and Pastoral Responses)

Even in healthy small groups, barriers to multiplication arise. These barriers often spring from the heart, fear of loss, insecurity, or misplaced priorities. Scripture speaks to each of these struggles and offers a gospel-shaped response.[166]

1. Comfort: "We'll miss our friends."

It is natural to grieve when people you love are sent to start something new. Yet multiplication is not abandonment; it is mission. Jesus said, *"As the Father has sent me, even so I am*

---

[166] See Bill Donahue and Russ Robinson, *Building a Church of Small Groups: A Place Where Nobody Stands Alone* (Grand Rapids: Zondervan, 2001); Dave Earley and Rod Dempsey, *Leading Healthy, Growing, Multiplying Small Groups* (Houston: Touch Outreach, 2010); J. Oswald Sanders, *Spiritual Leadership: Principles of Excellence for Every Believer*, rev. ed. (Chicago: Moody, 2007); Colin Marshall and Tony Payne, *The Trellis and the Vine: The Ministry Mind-Shift That Changes Everything* (Kingsford, Australia: Matthias Media, 2009); Steve Gladen, *Small Groups with Purpose: How to Create Healthy Communities* (Grand Rapids: Baker, 2011); Ken Braddy, "Four Qualities to Look for in Group Leaders," Ken Braddy: Sunday School Revolutionary, July 16, 2019, https://kenbraddy.com/2019/07/16/four-qualities-to-look-for-in-group-leaders/.

sending you" (John 20:21). Sending is an act of love, not rejection. Just as Paul and Barnabas returned to encourage the churches they had planted (Acts 14:21–23), groups can keep relational bridges alive through quarterly reunions or joint gatherings. Multiplication deepens, rather than diminishes, community by extending Christ's welcome to new people.

2. Control: "No one can lead like me."

Leaders sometimes fear releasing the reins. But Scripture reminds us that we are stewards, not owners. *"I planted, Apollos watered, but God gave the growth"* (1 Corinthians 3:6–7). The call of a leader is to equip others, not to cling tightly to authority (Ephesians 4:12). Healthy multiplication requires humility and trusting that Christ is the Chief Shepherd and that His Spirit equips every believer for ministry (1 Peter 5:2–4). When leaders release control, they mirror Jesus, who entrusted His mission to imperfect disciples and promised, *"I am with you always"* (Matthew 28:20).

3. Comparison: "I'm not as gifted."

Members may resist leadership because they feel inadequate. Yet Scripture assures us that *"there are varieties of gifts, but the same Spirit...To each is given the manifestation of the Spirit for the common good"* (1 Corinthians 12:4–7). God delights to use ordinary people to accomplish His extraordinary purposes. Paul reminded Timothy not to despise his youth but to *"fan into flame the gift of God"* (2 Timothy 1:6). New leaders can be paired with others and supported by a coach, modeling the biblical pattern of Barnabas mentoring Paul and Paul mentoring Timothy. Multiplication is not about equal gifting but about shared obedience.

4. Capacity: "I'm too busy to apprentice."

Busyness is a real challenge, but multiplication is not about adding a burden—it is about sharing one. Moses learned this when Jethro advised him to delegate responsibility; *"What you are doing is not good...You will certainly wear yourselves out"* (Exodus 18:17–18). Multiplication begins with small steps: letting someone lead prayer one week, handle follow-up the next. Jesus Himself gave responsibility in stages—first sending the Twelve (Luke 9:1–6), then the seventy-two (Luke 10:1–12). Small handoffs, done consistently, compound into leadership growth. The goal is not perfection but faithfulness with what God entrusts (Luke 16:10).

Multiplication will always stretch comfort zones, but it is the pathway of obedience. Each barrier, comfort, control, comparison, and capacity, finds its answer in Christ's Word and Holy Spirit. As leaders shepherd groups through these obstacles.[167]

A 12-Month Multiplication Roadmap (Example)

Quarter 1 — Pray & Identify

- Pray weekly for workers (Matthew 9:37–38).
- Observe CORE traits; invite one apprentice.

---

[167] Smith and Kai, *T4T*; Ferguson and Bird, *Hero Maker*; Braddy, "Why Multiplication Matters in Groups."

Quarter 2 — Train & Share

- Apprentice covers hospitality + prayer; you debrief monthly.
- Apprentice co-leads discussion twice.

Quarter 3 — Lead with Coaching

- Apprentice facilitates 50–75% of meetings; you coach.
- Communicate multiplication vision to the group; invite interest for the plant.

Quarter 4 — Launch & Support

- Commission the new group; send 4–6 volunteers.
- You (or a coach) shadow for the first 6–8 weeks, then quarterly thereafter.

Simple Tools You Can Use This Week

Apprentice Conversation Outline (30–45 minutes)

- **Scripture & prayer (10 minutes):** e.g., 2 Timothy 2:1–2; Matthew 28:19-20.
- **Debrief last meeting (10 minutes):** What went well? What would you change?
- **Skill focus (10 minutes):** Asking better questions / guiding prayer.
- **Plan & pray (5 minutes):** Who will you invest in this week?

Launching Checklist

- Clarify meeting when/where and child-care.
- Draft a four-week startup plan (welcome, Word, prayer, mission).
- Create simple contact & care rhythms (texts between meetings).
- Coordinate with church leadership for visibility and on-ramps.

Measuring What Matters

Healthy groups measure progress, not just numbers. Attendance is important, but it is only a lagging indicator—it tells you what has already happened. Far more valuable are leading indicators: inputs that leaders can influence and that reveal whether multiplication is actually taking root.

1. Apprentices Identified and Equipped: Every multiplying group should have apprentices actively being trained. This means more than naming someone—it means they are teaching periodically, meeting monthly with the leader, and being prepared to either lead the group or plant a new one. Apprentices are the clearest evidence that a group is serious about reproduction.

2. Shared Roles Rotating Regularly: Leadership is not meant to be hoarded. Healthy groups rotate responsibilities— hospitality, prayer, follow-up, mission projects—at least quarterly. This rotation builds ownership, prevents burnout, and reveals who is reliable and equippable (Luke 16:10; Ephesians 4:12).

3. Care and Mission Between Meetings: The true test of a group's health is what happens outside the meeting. Are members checking in, meeting needs, serving together, and sharing the gospel in their daily lives? When groups are living on mission between gatherings, multiplication becomes a natural overflow.

4. New Group Starts and Health Checks: Ultimately, multiplication means new groups. Tracking how many new groups launch each year matters, but so does their sustainability. A simple 30/60/90–day health check ensures that new groups are thriving in the Word, prayer, care, and mission, not just surviving.

5. **Spiritual and Relational Growth:** Finally, we must measure the less visible but most critical fruit: Are group members becoming more like Jesus (2 Corinthians 3:18)? Are relationships deepening in love, forgiveness, and accountability (John 13:34–35)? These cannot always be charted on a spreadsheet, but leaders can observe and celebrate them as true signs of multiplication.

In short, multiplication is not measured only by "how many attend" but by "how many are being equipped, sent, and transformed." If we measure what matters, we will multiply what matters.[168]

Multiplication Health Evaluation Form

This evaluation tool helps small group leaders assess the health of their group in multiplying leaders and groups on the following page. Use it quarterly to reflect on leading indicators

---

[168] Smith and Kai, *T4T*; Ferguson and Bird, *Hero Maker*; Braddy, "Why Multiplication Matters in Groups."

(inputs you can influence) and lagging indicators (outcomes over time). The following provides an indicator code on how to use this tool:

- **Green** = Healthy → Input is consistent and outcome is visible.
- **Yellow** = Growing → Input is present but not yet producing fruit.
- **Red** = Gap → Input missing or outcome stalling; requires leader attention.

Multiplication Health Dashboard

Category	Leading Indicators (Inputs to Track)	Track (Circle One)	Lagging Indicators (Fruit Over Time)
Leadership Development	Apprentices identified and meeting monthly and shared roles rotated quarterly.	Green Yellow Red	New leaders launched and groups multiplied.
Spiritual Growth	Members actively engaging Scripture and prayer. Testimonies of obedience and transformation are being shared.	Green Yellow Red	Evident Christlike character (Gal. 5:22-23)
Care & Mission	Members checking in, providing care outside group. They are serving together in community or mission projects.	Green Yellow Red	Ongoing culture of discipleship and outreach
Relational Health	Guests welcomed and followed up within 72 hours. The group has regular fellowships or meals together.	Green Yellow Red	Stronger connections, reduced dropouts
Group Reproduction	New group plans identified (apprentice ready, launch date set). There is a 30/60/90–day health check-ins scheduled.	Green Yellow Red	Sustainable new groups started each year

Frequently Asked Questions[169]

Q: "Won't launching a new group hurt our current group's relationships?"

A: It may feel like multiplication will take away the closeness you've built. But in reality, it preserves the health of your group. A small group that never multiplies risks becoming inward-focused. Multiplying ensures that mission and welcome stay at the center. In Acts 11:19–26, believers shared the gospel in new places, and instead of losing fellowship, their community grew stronger and wider. Sending people out doesn't end community; it extends it, creating new circles of friendship and discipleship.

Q: "What if the new group fails?"

A: Sometimes a new group struggles or even dissolves. That's okay. Small groups are places of growth, not perfection. Proverbs 24:16 reminds us that the righteous fall and rise again. Even if a new group doesn't last, nothing is wasted. Those who stepped out to lead gain experience, and the parent group learns what to adjust next time. Keep praying, keep coaching, and try again. Every attempt is a step of obedience that God uses to grow both leaders and groups.

Q: "How do we keep the vision for multiplication alive in our group?"

A: Vision fades unless it is refreshed. Small group leaders can keep the vision alive by weaving it into the group's life:

---

[169] Smith and Kai, *T4T*; Ferguson and Bird, *Hero Maker*; Braddy, "Why Multiplication Matters in Groups."

- Share fresh stories of other groups multiplying.
- Celebrate when members take steps of leadership.
- Regularly revisit key Scriptures like 2 Timothy 2:2 (entrusting truth to faithful people), Matthew 28:18–20 (the Great Commission), and Acts 2:42–47 (gospel-centered community that kept spreading).

When a group regularly hears why multiplication matters and sees it celebrated, it learns to view multiplication not as loss but as legacy.

Q: "What if some members resist multiplying?"

A: It's natural for members to feel nervous about change. They've built trust and don't want to lose it. The role of the leader is to shepherd patiently. Teach that multiplication doesn't mean losing relationships—it means widening the circle so that others can belong. In Luke 10:1, Jesus sent disciples out in pairs, not because they had exhausted fellowship, but because the harvest was ready. Encourage members to view multiplication as generosity: they are sharing what they've enjoyed with others who still need it.

Q: "How do we know when our small group is ready to multiply?"

A: Readiness is less about perfection and more about health. A small group may be ready to multiply when:

- An apprentice leader has been identified and trained.
- The group has developed consistent rhythms of Word, prayer, and fellowship.
- Members understand the "why" of multiplication and are willing, even if hesitant.

- There is ongoing support and coaching for the new leader.

The best time is rarely when everything feels "just right." Groups multiply by faith, trusting that God sustains His people as they step out in obedience.

Q: "How do we keep relationships strong after multiplying?"

A: One of the biggest fears is losing friendships. But multiplication doesn't mean disconnection. Encourage groups to keep relationships alive by:

- Planning occasional joint gatherings (meals, service projects, socials).
- Staying connected through texts or prayer chains.
- Continuing to celebrate milestones together (birthdays, baptisms, answered prayers). Remember, multiplication changes meeting rhythms, but it doesn't erase friendships.

Q: "How do we prepare an apprentice leader without overwhelming them?"

A: Raising leaders happens gradually. Start by giving small responsibilities—leading prayer, organizing fellowship, or contacting absent members. Over time, let the apprentice lead a discussion while you coach. Acts 18:26 gives a picture of Priscilla and Aquila gently guiding Apollos as he grew in leadership. Keep leadership development relational and encouraging, not rushed or pressured.

Q: "What if my group is too small to multiply?"

A: Even smaller groups can multiply in creative ways. Consider forming triads or quads for a season, where a few people meet separately for deeper discipleship and then return to the main group. Over time, one of these smaller gatherings can grow into a full group. The goal isn't numbers, it's developing disciples who can disciple others.

Conclusion

Multiplication is the overflow of Christ's life in His people. As groups form disciples, develop leaders, and send new groups, the church grows up into Christ and out toward the world (Ephesians 4:15–16). This is not loss—it is legacy (1 Corinthians 3:6–9).

Reflection & Action

1. Name one apprentice you will invite this month.

2. Name two roles you will hand off in the next four weeks.

3. Name one opportunity (place/people/time) where a new group could start.

4. Set a sending date window (Quarter 3 or 4) and put two coaching check-ins on the calendar.

Conclusion of Part 3: Practices for Healthy Groups

Healthy small groups are not accidental, they are cultivated with clarity, order, care, and multiplication. In this section, we have seen that leaders must clarify the purpose so groups stay on mission and avoid drift (Acts 2:42–47). They must also establish practical organization, because *"all things should be done decently and in order"* (1 Corinthians 14:40), creating reproducible rhythms that free the Spirit to work. Beyond structure, leaders are called to pastoral care, embodying the Good Shepherd by knowing, guiding, protecting, and feeding the flock entrusted to them (John 10:11; 1 Peter 5:2–3). Finally, healthy groups embrace multiplication, raising apprentices who will carry the mission forward to new people and places.

When these practices come together, groups move from being simple gatherings to becoming spiritual families on mission—places where disciples are formed, leaders are raised, and the kingdom of God is extended. The call of Jesus was never just to gather but to go, to make disciples who make disciples (Matthew 28:18–20). Part 3 has given us the practical pathways to live this out.

As we turn to the next section, we will see how these practices take root in real time through consistent habits and rhythms that allow groups to thrive for the long haul.

Part 4: Challenges and Encouragement

Chapter 12: Mission

"By this all people will know that you are my disciples, if you have love for one another." — (John 13:35, ESV)

Small groups are never meant to be holy huddles as mentioned in earlier chapters. While fellowship and care are essential, discipleship without mission quickly becomes ingrown. Jesus' Great Commission calls every believer and every group outward: *"Go therefore and make disciples of all nations, baptizing them in the name of the Father and of the Son and of the Holy Spirit, teaching them to observe all that I have commanded you. And behold, I am with you always, to the end of the age"* (Matt. 28:19–20, ESV).

From Vertical to Horizontal

As someone who has observed small group ministries across many churches, one of my first tasks is often helping groups move from an inward focus to an upward focus. When small groups are centered only on themselves, they risk becoming "holy huddles." However, when groups lift their eyes upward toward God, it naturally bends their perspective outward toward others. Jesus taught this principle clearly: when our relationship with Him is healthy and vibrant vertically, it will overflow horizontally into our relationships with people.

This outward expression is not limited to serving in the community, though that is certainly part of it. It also shapes how we treat one another within the group and within the church family. Love, encouragement, accountability, and care become tangible when the group lives missionally. But the group's mission should always align with the greater mission of the local church. That's why it is vital for leaders to talk with their pastor, ask about the vision the Lord has placed on his heart, and explore ways the group can partner with existing church ministries. A small group that embraces the larger mission of its church will not only grow spiritually but also multiply its impact.

Jesus summarized the entire law with two great commandments: to love God (vertical) and to love others (horizontal) (Matthew 22:37–40). A vertical love for God naturally spills outward to people. When groups cultivate a Christ-centered outlook, their relationships extend beyond themselves and become a visible witness. John 13:35 reminds us that love within the church is itself evangelistic—*"By this all people will know that you are my disciples, if you have love for one another."* That inward love becomes a testimony to the world.

But the call does not stop there. Acts 1:8 shows the outward trajectory of God's mission from Jerusalem to Judea, to Samaria, and to the ends of the earth. The early church did not remain inward or stationary; they multiplied leadership, sent believers into new places, and carried the gospel outward. In the same way, when small groups are anchored upward in Christ, they will inevitably move outward on mission. The vertical relationship fuels the horizontal expression, and together they form the heartbeat of biblical community.[170]

From Holy Huddle to Gospel Witness

We cannot be satisfied with simply staying where we are or settling into comfort. It is far too easy for groups to become inwardly focused, enjoying fellowship and familiarity without ever lifting their eyes to the mission of God. A small group that only looks inward risks becoming what some call a "holy huddle." Which is a safe, comfortable, and even enjoyable, but ultimately a stagnant group. When groups forget their outward call, they miss half their purpose.

True disciple-making communities do not stop at personal growth; they turn outward in love for their neighbors, coworkers, classmates, and communities. Evangelism and discipleship are not competing tasks—they are two sides of the same coin. A group that takes discipleship seriously will eventually be propelled into evangelism, because a disciple who is growing in Christ will naturally want to share Christ. Likewise, evangelism must lead into discipleship, for those

---

[170] See Christopher J. H. Wright, *The Mission of God: Unlocking the Bible's Grand Narrative* (Downers Grove, IL: IVP Academic, 2006); Ed Stetzer and Eric Geiger, *Transformational Groups: Creating a New Scorecard for Groups* (Nashville: B&H Publishing, 2014); Rosaria Butterfield, *The Gospel Comes with a House Key: Practicing Radically Ordinary Hospitality in Our Post-Christian World* (Wheaton, IL: Crossway, 2018); David J. Bosch, *Transforming Mission: Paradigm Shifts in Theology of Mission* (Maryknoll, NY: Orbis Books, 1991); Alan Hirsch, *The Forgotten Ways: Reactivating the Missional Church* (Grand Rapids: Brazos, 2006); Ken Braddy, "Groups on Mission: Why Small Groups Must Live Sent," Ken Braddy Blog, Lifeway, accessed September 27, 2025, https://kenbraddy.com.

who hear the gospel need to be nurtured in faith and trained in obedience. Both belong together in the life of a healthy small group.

Leaders play a vital role in helping their groups see themselves not as consumers of ministry but as participants in God's mission. This means continually asking: How are we growing deeper in Christ together, and how are we reaching farther for Christ together? When groups wrestle with these questions, they begin to see that their purpose is not just to care for each other, but also to become gospel witnesses in the world around them.

The church in Antioch is a great case study of this posture (Acts 11:19–26). Ordinary believers who had been scattered preached the gospel faithfully, and as people believed, the church was strengthened. Barnabas was sent to encourage them, and under his leadership, the church quickly grew into the first great missionary-sending hub of the New Testament. From Antioch, missionaries like Paul and Barnabas were commissioned to take the gospel to the nations. What began with everyday believers sharing Jesus with others turned into a movement that shaped the entire course of church history.

Small groups today can embody that same Antioch spirit. When groups encourage one another in the Word, build each other up in love, and then intentionally step outside their walls to serve, share, and send, they transform from being holy huddles into gospel outposts. They become not only places of community but also launching pads for mission.[171]

---

[171] Wright, *Mission of God*; Stetzer and Geiger, *Transformational Groups;* Butterfield, *Gospel Comes with a House Key*; Bosch, *Transforming Mission;* Hirsch, *The Forgotten Ways*; Braddy, "Groups on Mission."

Groups as Evangelistic Outposts

Every small group is a frontline gospel witness. Homes become mission outposts when doors are opened to seekers and friends. Rosaria Butterfield writes, "Radically ordinary hospitality is this: using your Christian home in a daily way that seeks to make strangers neighbors, and neighbors family of God."[172]

The table where discipleship happens can also be the table where unbelievers encounter grace. In Acts 9, Barnabas welcomed Saul when others were hesitant. In Acts 16, Lydia opened her home to Paul and Silas, and her entire household believed. In Acts 18, Priscilla and Aquila took Apollos aside and discipled him more fully. Each example demonstrates how homes and groups can become gospel outposts. Is your home a gospel outpost? Is your small group a gospel outpost?

Practical Ways to Live On Mission as a Small Group

Practical ways to live missionally as a group are both simple and impactful. One way is through **service projects**, such as adopting a classroom, serving at a homeless shelter, volunteering at a pregnancy center, or partnering with a local mission effort. These opportunities help groups step outside themselves and demonstrate Christ's love in tangible ways.

---

[172] Rosaria Butterfield, The Gospel Comes with a House Key: Practicing Radically Ordinary Hospitality in Our Post-Christian World (Wheaton, IL: Crossway, 2018), 31.

Another practice is engaging in **prayer walks**, where members walk through neighborhoods together, praying over homes and asking God to open hearts. This intentional intercession not only blesses the community but also reminds the group that God is at work beyond their gathering space.

Hospitality is also a powerful tool for mission. By sharing meals, hosting community nights, or inviting neighbors into the natural rhythm of the group, believers open their lives in a way that reflects the welcome of Christ. Hospitality often provides the first step toward meaningful gospel conversations.

In addition, groups should train members to have **gospel conversations**—learning to share personal testimonies and present the gospel naturally through tools such as the 3 Circles or the Romans Road. These simple practices help believers grow in confidence and obedience to Christ's call to make disciples.

Finally, groups can build **missional rhythms** into their gatherings by dedicating time each month for members to share outreach stories and pray specifically for lost friends and family. These rhythms keep mission at the forefront and cultivate a culture where living sent is the norm, not the exception.

The Great Commission Lens

As a group leader, it's important to pause and ask: Am I looking at my group through the lens of the Great Commission? Jesus' final command wasn't simply to gather, but to *"make disciples of all nations"* (Matthew 28:19–20). This means every small group should be more than a Bible discussion or social circle; it should be a training ground and launching pad for obedience, mission, and multiplication. When we see through the Great Commission lens, we move from:

- Application → Action
- Comfort → Commission
- Seats → Streets
- Program → People

A Great Commission group is not content to sit idly and remain stagnant. Instead, it equips members to live sent lives in their workplaces, schools, neighborhoods, and homes. In my experience, it is harder to move a stagnant group toward mission, especially if they have been established and are satisfied where they are. This is where the leader must step in to ensure the group begins to view things through a missional lens. That lens is not limited to financial support for missions; it reflects an active posture of the heart.[173]

Three Key Questions for Leaders

Moving a group toward a Great Commission lens is a key responsibility for every small group leader. A group is not healthy if it only gathers inwardly without looking outward to mission. To help you discern where your group stands, ask yourself the following questions:

- **Does our study lead to obedience?**
  Bible study is not complete until it leads to obedience. James reminds us, *"Be doers of the word, and not hearers only"* (James 1:22). A Great Commission lens

---

[173] Wright, *Mission of God*; Stetzer and Geiger, *Transformational Groups;* Butterfield, *Gospel Comes with a House Key*; Bosch, *Transforming Mission;* Hirsch, *The Forgotten Ways*; Braddy, "Groups on Mission."

means your group doesn't stop with good discussion; it presses forward into real-life obedience. Are your members walking away with clear steps to live out what they've studied?

- **Does our fellowship stir courage to witness?**
  Christian fellowship should not just comfort but also embolden. Hebrews 10:24–25 tells us to *"stir one another up to love and good works."* In a culture often hostile to the gospel, believers need encouragement from one another to share their faith. Ask: is your group challenging one another to love boldly, speak truthfully, and engage missionally?

- **Does our prayer life include intercession for the lost?**
  A Great Commission group prays outwardly. Paul urged believers to pray *"for all people…that they may be saved"* (1 Timothy 2:1–4). Does your group regularly name lost friends, family, and neighbors before God? Prayer aligns our hearts with God's mission and fuels courage to step into gospel conversations.

The Perspective Shift

Groups aligned with the Great Commission will not settle for comfort, they will embrace the call to make disciples. This means measuring "success" not by how many people attend, but by how many are sent. It means viewing your living room not only as a gathering space, but as a launching pad.

The Great Commission lens keeps groups from becoming self-focused or stagnant. Instead, they become gospel outposts, places where people are equipped, encouraged, and then released to live sent lives.

As a leader, remember: your group isn't just a circle of chairs; it's part of the global mission of God. Mission naturally leads to multiplication. As groups reach new people, they outgrow their circle and need to multiply into new groups. Evangelism fuels expansion, and expansion fuels evangelism.[174]

Practical Steps Toward Mission Focus Small Groups

Practical steps can help any small group shift from an inward focus to an outward, mission-oriented posture. Step one is to **begin every group meeting with prayer** for lost friends and family. By keeping a written list and revisiting it regularly, members hold one another accountable and keep evangelism at the forefront of group life. This practice reminds everyone that mission begins with intercession and depends on the work of God's Spirit.

Step two is to **serve together regularly in a community or service project**. Whether it's helping at a local school, volunteering at a food pantry, or supporting a pregnancy center, shared service bonds the group while putting Christ's love into action. Serving side by side often opens doors for gospel conversations and strengthens relationships within the group.

Step three is to **train members in a simple gospel tool**. Approaches such as the 3 Circles, Romans Road, or a personal testimony outline provide confidence and clarity for sharing the

---

[174] Wright, *Mission of God*; Stetzer and Geiger, *Transformational Groups;* Butterfield, *Gospel Comes with a House Key*; Bosch, *Transforming Mission;* Hirsch, *The Forgotten Ways*; Braddy, "Groups on Mission."

good news. When every member feels equipped, mission becomes less intimidating and more natural.

Step four is to **celebrate gospel conversations and testimonies**. Taking time during group gatherings to share these stories builds faith, fuels courage, and reminds members that God is at work through them. Celebration creates a culture where evangelism is both expected and encouraged.

Finally, step five is to **partner with global missions by adopting missionaries or projects**. Praying for specific missionaries, writing letters of encouragement, or raising support for projects connects the group to God's worldwide mission. This widens the group's vision beyond their neighborhood and shows that they are part of the Great Commission movement stretching to the ends of the earth.

Together, these five steps move small groups from passive gatherings to active gospel outposts. They help members grow deeper in Christ while reaching farther for His kingdom.[175]

Conclusion

When small groups embrace mission, they cease to be optional programs on a church calendar. They become the living heartbeat of the Great Commission. Groups no longer exist simply for convenience or community; they exist for calling. In living rooms, coffee shops, and break rooms, groups step beyond the walls of the church and into the lives of people who may never set foot in a sanctuary.

------

[175] Wright, *Mission of God*; Stetzer and Geiger, *Transformational Groups;* Butterfield, *Gospel Comes with a House Key*; Bosch, *Transforming Mission;* Hirsch, *The Forgotten Ways*; Braddy, "Groups on Mission."

Missional small groups are frontline ministries. They reach neighbors, coworkers, and classmates with the gospel in ways pastors may never be able to. Through relationships, meals, acts of service, and Spirit-led conversations, groups embody the presence of Christ in everyday life. They carry the mission of the church into spaces sermons cannot reach and shepherd hearts that formal programs cannot always touch.

This outward posture is not an optional add-on—it is central to obedience. Jesus' call to *"make disciples of all nations"* (Matthew 28:19) was not given only to pastors or missionaries, but to every believer. Small groups that embrace this call become multiplying centers of disciple-making: places where people are taught to obey Christ, where new leaders are raised up, and where the gospel naturally flows outward into communities and beyond.

When groups embrace mission, they redefine success. Success is not measured by how many attend but by how many are sent. It is not about keeping people comfortable but about sending people courageous. A missional group becomes both a family of disciples and a force for disciple-making—reflecting the very design of the church itself. In the end, groups aligned with the Great Commission remind us that mission is not something the church does; mission is who the church is.

Reflective Questions

1. Does my group pray consistently for lost people by name?

2. Have we built rhythms of service and evangelism into our gatherings?

3. Are we celebrating gospel conversations as much as answered personal prayers?

4. If our group dissolved today, would our community even notice?

5. Do our meetings reflect both the vertical (love for God) and the horizontal (love for others)?

6. How is our group serving as a gospel outpost in our neighborhood, school, or workplace?

7. What specific mission field (homeless, children, widows, internationals, etc.) is God placing before us right now?

8. How can we structure our group to multiply, not just maintain?

Chapter 13: Challenges and Conflict

"If possible, so far as it depends on you, live peaceably with all" (Romans 12:18, ESV).

The Reality of Conflict

Every small group will face challenges. Conflict is not a possibility; it is a certainty, because groups are made up of people who still wrestle with sin. Even followers of Jesus, redeemed by His grace, remain imperfect in this life. That's why Scripture doesn't ignore conflict; it directly addresses it. Jesus gave instructions in Matthew 18, Paul urged churches toward unity in Ephesians 4, and James warned against quarrels rooted in selfish desires (James 4:1).

The real question is not if conflict comes, but how we respond when it does. Healthy groups face challenges biblically, allowing conflict to become a refining tool that deepens trust and points people back to Christ. Ignoring problems only lets bitterness grow, but handling them God's way produces reconciliation and stronger fellowship.[176]

Common Challenges in Small Groups

Small groups often encounter a variety of challenges that can hinder their health and effectiveness. One common difficulty is the presence of dominating members. These individuals may consistently control the conversation, unintentionally limiting others from participating. Scripture reminds us, *"Let every person be quick to hear, slow to speak"* (James 1:19). Leaders can handle this by graciously acknowledging the person's input while redirecting the discussion and intentionally inviting quieter voices to share. This approach values the individual but also ensures that the whole group has room to contribute.

On the other end of the spectrum, some groups struggle with silent members. Whether due to shyness, fear, or lack of confidence, these individuals may remain quiet even when they have valuable perspectives to offer. The Bible exhorts us to *"encourage one another and build one another up"* (1 Thessalonians 5:11). Leaders can foster participation by gently drawing them out with open-ended questions, using smaller

---

[176] See Ken Sande, *The Peacemaker: A Biblical Guide to Resolving Personal Conflict* (Grand Rapids: Baker Books, 2004); Alfred Poirier, *The Peacemaking Pastor: A Biblical Guide to Resolving Church Conflict* (Grand Rapids: Baker Books, 2006); Jim Van Yperen, *Making Peace: A Guide to Overcoming Church Conflict* (Chicago: Moody Publishers, 2002); Marshall Shelley, *Well-Intentioned Dragons: Ministering to Problem People in the Church* (Minneapolis: Bethany House, 1994); Ken Braddy, "Handling Conflict in Your Group," Ken Braddy Blog, Lifeway, accessed September 27, 2025, https://kenbraddy.com.

breakouts, or affirming even brief contributions. Over time, a culture of encouragement helps hesitant members find their voice.

Another challenge is inconsistent attendance. Busy schedules, family responsibilities, or waning commitment can cause members to drift, weakening the group's sense of community. Hebrews urges us not to neglect meeting together but to *"stir up one another to love and good works"* (Hebrews 10:24–25). Rather than responding with guilt, leaders should reach out with care, reminding absent members of the group's value and encouraging their continued involvement.

Small groups are also affected by personal crises within their members. Illness, grief, or financial struggles can weigh heavily on individuals and the group as a whole. Scripture calls us to *"bear one another's burdens, and so fulfill the law of Christ"* (Galatians 6:2). In these times, groups should rally together through prayer, presence, and tangible support, such as providing meals, visits, financial help, or simply a listening ear. Such care turns trials into opportunities for the group to live out the love of Christ.

Finally, interpersonal conflict is an inevitable reality in community life. Misunderstandings, offenses, or gossip can create division if left unresolved. Jesus gave clear guidance: *"If your brother sins against you, go and tell him his fault, between you and him alone"* (Matthew 18:15). Leaders should encourage members to handle issues directly, with humility and love, rather than involving others unnecessarily. Truth spoken in love not only restores broken relationships but also strengthens the group's witness to the power of the gospel.[177]

---

[177] See Sande, *Peacemaker*; Poirier, *Peacemaking Pastor*; Braddy, "Handling Conflict in Your Group."

Handling Conflict Biblically: The Matthew 18 Principle

Conflict is unavoidable in Christian community, but Jesus did not leave His disciples without guidance. In Matthew 18:15–17, He gave the church a clear, Spirit-led process for handling conflict. This principle is not about punishment or power, it is about restoration, reconciliation, and protecting the unity of the body of Christ.[178]

1. Go Privately: Jesus said, *"If your brother sins against you, go and tell him his fault, between you and him alone"* (Matthew 18:15). The first step is always personal, not public. Running to others spreads gossip and breeds division. By addressing the issue one-on-one, leaders and members give space for repentance, forgiveness, and reconciliation without unnecessary embarrassment. Proverbs reminds us, *"Hatred stirs up strife, but love covers all offenses"* (Proverbs 10:12). Private, prayerful conversation is the way love covers.

2. Bring Others if Needed: If resolution is not found, Jesus instructs, *"But if he does not listen, take one or two others along with you, that every charge may be established by the evidence of two or three witnesses"* (Matthew 18:16). This step is not about building a case but about seeking wise counsel and accountability. Others can help clarify the issue, confirm truth, and encourage reconciliation. Ecclesiastes reminds us of the strength of unity: *"Two are better than one...and a threefold cord is not quickly broken"* (Ecclesiastes 4:9–12). Involving others creates a circle of grace and truth rather than escalating tension.

---

[178] See Sande, *Peacemaker*; Poirier, *Peacemaking Pastor*; Braddy, "Handling Conflict in Your Group."

3. Involve Leadership: If reconciliation is still refused, Jesus says, *"If he refuses to listen to them, tell it to the church"* (Matthew 18:17). At this point, church leadership becomes involved, not to condemn, but to shepherd. Leaders bear the responsibility of guarding the flock (Acts 20:28). The aim is still restoration, not punishment. Paul echoes this spirit when he writes, *"Brothers, if anyone is caught in any transgression, you who are spiritual should restore him in a spirit of gentleness"* (Galatians 6:1). Even when conflict reaches the highest levels, the posture must remain one of grace-filled restoration.

The Matthew 18 principle makes it clear: the goal is always to *"gain your brother"* (Matthew 18:15). Biblical conflict resolution is never about "winning" an argument but about winning back a relationship. Leaders must model humility, grace, and courage, remembering that Christ reconciled us to Himself when we were His enemies (Romans 5:10). If He pursued us with patient love, we are called to do the same for one another.[179]

A Biblical Perspective on Conflict

Conflict is not foreign to the pages of Scripture. From Genesis to Revelation, we see people wrestling with disagreements, tensions, and broken relationships. Yet God, in His wisdom, shows us how to deal with conflict in ways that both honor Him and advance His mission.

Even among godly leaders, disagreement arose. Paul and Barnabas experienced a "sharp disagreement" in Acts 15:36–41 over John Mark. Though painful, God used it to multiply

---

[179] Kent Shepherd, *The Barnabas Factor: A Guide to Discipleship Leadership* (Steens, MS: Shepherd Ministry Resources, 2025), 137–39.

missionary teams, Barnabas mentoring John Mark, and Paul choosing Silas to strengthen the churches. What looked like division, God turned into multiplication. This reminds us that conflict, when surrendered to Christ, can serve His purposes and expand the gospel witness.

Paul later urged believers: *"I entreat Euodia and I entreat Syntyche to agree in the Lord"* (Philippians 4:2). He didn't ignore their tension; he called them to gospel-centered unity. Rather than letting strife linger, Paul pressed them toward reconciliation because unresolved conflict damages both the witness of the church and the joy of its members.

Jesus Himself addressed conflict directly. In Matthew 18:15–17, He laid out a process of going first to a brother or sister privately, then involving others if necessary, always with the aim of restoration. Conflict avoidance is never the biblical answer; love requires courageous engagement. *"Blessed are the peacemakers,"* Jesus said, *"for they shall be called sons of God"* (Matthew 5:9).

James reminds us of the heart-level nature of conflict: *"What causes quarrels and what causes fights among you? Is it not this, that your passions are at war within you?"* (James 4:1). Many conflicts stem not just from surface disagreements but from competing desires. This calls small group leaders to shepherd hearts, not merely to manage conversations.

Small groups, like the early church, are called to pursue reconciliation rooted in Christ's love. Colossians 3:13 exhorts believers to *"bear with one another and, if one has a complaint against another, forgiving each other; as the Lord has forgiven you, so you also must forgive."* Forgiveness is the gospel lived out in community.

When handled biblically, conflict becomes an opportunity for discipleship. Leaders can model humility, patience, listening, and truth spoken in love (Ephesians 4:15). Rather than tearing apart, conflict can refine relationships, strengthen unity, and magnify the grace of Christ.[180]

The Leader's Posture

A small group leader is not called to act as a referee, blowing the whistle on every disagreement, but as a shepherd, guiding people toward Christ and His peace. The posture of the heart matters as much as the words spoken. Scripture gives us a clear framework for how leaders are to walk when conflict arises.[181]

- **Prayerful Posture:** Before addressing any issue, leaders are to seek the Lord in prayer. Paul exhorts, *"Do not be anxious about anything, but in everything by prayer and supplication with thanksgiving let your requests be made known to God"* (Philippians 4:6). Conflict easily stirs anxiety, but prayer shifts the burden to God, and His peace guards both heart and mind (Philippians 4:7). Leaders must begin on their knees before stepping into difficult conversations.

- **Truth in Love:** Biblical leadership never avoids truth, but it also never separates truth from love. Paul reminds us to be *"speaking the truth in love, [so that] we are to grow up in every way into him who is the head, into Christ"* (Ephesians 4:15). Words spoken harshly can

---

[180] Kent Shepherd, *The Barnabas Factor: A Guide to Discipleship Leadership* (Steens, MS: Shepherd Ministry Resources, 2025), 137–39.

[181] See Sande, *Peacemaker*; Poirier, *Peacemaking Pastor*; Braddy, "Handling Conflict in Your Group."

wound, while love without truth compromises holiness. The balance of honesty and compassion allows conflict to become a pathway for spiritual growth rather than division.

- **Gentleness:** Conflict resolution demands humility, not harshness. Paul writes that *"the Lord's servant must not be quarrelsome but kind to everyone, able to teach, patiently enduring evil, correcting his opponents with gentleness"* (2 Timothy 2:24–25). Gentleness is not weakness, it is Holy Spirit-empowered strength under control. Leaders model Christ, who said, *"I am gentle and lowly in heart"* (Matthew 11:29), when they approach others with patience and compassion.

- **Timeliness:** Allowing wounds to fester only deepens division. Hebrews warns, *"See to it that no one fails to obtain the grace of God; that no root of bitterness springs up and causes trouble, and by it many become defiled"* (Hebrews 12:15). A leader who procrastinates or avoids addressing conflict risks allowing bitterness to spread within the group. Shepherds must courageously deal with issues promptly, before small fractures become lasting rifts.

Above all, leaders must first examine their own hearts. Jesus taught, *"First take the log out of your own eye, and then you will see clearly to take the speck out of your brother's eye"* (Matthew 7:5). Leaders cannot guide others toward reconciliation if they are unwilling to submit their own attitudes, motives, and words to the Lord. Only then can they lead their group into Christlike resolution that honors God and restores unity.[182]

Practical Tools for Groups

Healthy small groups can prepare for challenges before they arise by establishing practical tools that create a strong foundation. One essential step is **establishing ground rules**. These should include commitments to confidentiality, respect, and active listening. When group members know they can share openly without fear of gossip or dismissal, trust grows and relationships deepen. Clear expectations at the outset prevent confusion and provide a standard to return to when tensions surface.

Another important tool is **promoting direct communication**. Conflict often escalates when issues are discussed about people rather than with them. Leaders should encourage members to go directly to one another when concerns arise, reflecting Jesus' teaching in Matthew 18:15. This practice not only prevents gossip but also fosters maturity, honesty, and grace-filled relationships.

Groups may also benefit from creating a **conflict covenant**, a shared commitment to handle disagreements biblically. Such a covenant reminds members that problems should not be ignored or whispered about but addressed in a spirit of love and restoration. By setting this expectation in advance, groups are better prepared to walk through inevitable tensions with unity and integrity.

---

[182] See Sande, *Peacemaker*; Poirier, *Peacemaking Pastor*; Braddy, "Handling Conflict in Your Group."

Finally, leaders must discern **when to escalate** conflict beyond the group. While many issues can and should be resolved within the circle, there are times when pastoral leadership must be involved, such as cases of divisive behavior, unrepentant sin, or potential harm. Titus 3:10 warns about those who persist in stirring division, and wise leaders protect the group by seeking pastoral guidance in such situations. Knowing when to seek outside help safeguards the health of both the group and the wider church body.

Taken together, these practical tools equip small groups not only to handle conflict but to grow stronger through it. By preparing in advance, groups cultivate an atmosphere of trust, accountability, and biblical love that enables them to thrive even when challenges come (see Appendix 4).

Encouragement for the Weary Leader

Conflict is exhausting. Leaders often carry not only their own burdens but also the tensions within the group. At times, this weight can feel overwhelming, leading shepherds to question if the effort is worth it. Yet God promises strength for those who remain faithful. He reminds us, *"My grace is sufficient for you, for my power is made perfect in weakness"* (2 Corinthians 12:9). In moments of fatigue, His grace sustains where human strength fails.

Scripture repeatedly assures weary leaders that perseverance in trial produces blessing. James exhorts believers to *"count it all joy…when you meet trials of various kinds, for you know that the testing of your faith produces steadfastness"* (James 1:2–3). Conflict, though draining, can be God's tool for shaping steadfast leaders who are *"perfect and complete, lacking in nothing"* (James 1:4).

Jesus Himself offers comfort to those weighed down by leadership struggles. *"Come to me, all who labor and are heavy laden, and I will give you rest"* (Matthew 11:28). Small group leaders must remember that their first role is not to carry every burden alone, but to continually rest in Christ. He walks with His servants, refreshing their souls even in seasons of strain (Psalm 23:1–3).

Paul's example also encourages weary leaders. In Galatians 6:9 he writes, *"And let us not grow weary of doing good, for in due season we will reap, if we do not give up."* Conflict resolution is part of *"doing good"* for the body of Christ. Though results may not be immediate, perseverance bears fruit in God's timing.

Leaders who endure conflict with faith not only protect their group's unity but also embody what it means to walk in the Spirit. Their patience, gentleness, and steadfast love demonstrate Christlike character (Galatians 5:22–23) and serve as a living testimony to their group.

The path of shepherding is not without strain, but it is never without reward. God sees the unseen labor of faithful leaders (Hebrews 6:10), and in Christ, no effort to preserve His flock is wasted.[183]

Conclusion

Conflict is inevitable, but it is not terminal. In fact, Scripture reminds us that disagreements, though often uncomfortable, can become holy ground for transformation when handled with humility and obedience to Christ. Healthy

---

[183] See Sande, *Peacemaker*; Poirier, *Peacemaking Pastor*; Braddy, "Handling Conflict in Your Group."

small groups do not view conflict as the end of fellowship but as an invitation to grow deeper in grace.

When we submit conflict to God's Word and Spirit, it shifts from being a destructive force to a refining process. Disagreements can sharpen our love, test our patience, and deepen our understanding of the gospel. As Paul wrote, *"If possible, so far as it depends on you, live peaceably with all"* (Romans 12:18). The goal is never to "win" an argument but to honor Christ by seeking reconciliation and unity.

Small groups that learn to face challenges with prayer, forgiveness, and courage become stronger witnesses to the world. Jesus said, *"By this all people will know that you are my disciples, if you have love for one another"* (John 13:35). Love is most visible not when everything is easy, but when grace prevails in the midst of difficulty.

Conflict, when handled biblically, becomes an opportunity for growth, reconciliation, and deeper discipleship. Healthy groups don't run from tension—they redeem it for the glory of Christ.

Reflective Questions

1. Am I more likely to avoid conflict or to address it too harshly? How does Scripture call me to balance truth and love?

2. When was the last time I saw conflict strengthen rather than weaken a relationship? What can I learn from that?

3. Do I encourage my group members to go directly to one another in disagreements, or do I allow gossip to grow?

4. How do I personally model humility when I am wrong or misunderstood in the group?
5. What steps can I take now to prepare my group for handling conflict biblically when it arises?

6. Am I relying on my own wisdom to navigate conflict, or am I daily seeking the Spirit's guidance?

Conclusion: Faithful Leadership in Small Groups

Small group leaders carry a sacred trust. They are not simply facilitators of meetings but shepherds of souls, stewards of God's Word, and multipliers of disciple-makers. The New Testament vision of leadership is never about power or position but about service. Jesus said, *"Whoever would be great among you must be your servant, and whoever would be first among you must be slave of all. For even the Son of Man came not to be served but to serve, and to give his life as a ransom for many"* (Mark 10:43–45, ESV).

Healthy small groups rise or fall on the faithfulness of their leaders. A leader's character, dependence on Scripture, and surrender to the Holy Spirit shape the culture of the group and ripple outward into the church and community. This calling is not to be taken lightly, but neither is it to be borne alone—God supplies grace, the Spirit empowers, and the church stands alongside those who lead.

Leaders as Servants, Shepherds, and Multipliers

Servants: Faithful leaders follow Christ's example of humility. They do not lead for applause but to build up others. Like Jesus washing His disciples' feet (John 13:12–15), leaders embody servant leadership by choosing presence over platform and sacrifice over self.

Shepherds: Leaders watch over the flock entrusted to them (1 Peter 5:2–3). They intercede in prayer, encourage the discouraged, and guide their people with biblical wisdom. Shepherding means walking with members through both joy and sorrow, pointing them continually to Christ, the Chief Shepherd (John 10:11).

Multipliers: Leaders embrace the Barnabas-to-Paul-to-Timothy model (Acts 11; 2 Timothy 2:2). They pour into apprentices, raise up new leaders, and release groups to multiply. Healthy small group leaders refuse to hoard influence; instead, they invest in others so that the church grows stronger and the gospel spreads further.[184]

Small Groups as Discipleship Engines for the Church

When small groups are healthy, they function as the primary discipleship engines of the local church. In living rooms, classrooms, and coffee shops, God shapes character, deepens relationships, and mobilizes His people for mission.

The Sunday gathering proclaims the Word and unites the body, but the smaller gathering applies the Word and personalizes care. Together, they form the rhythm of church life—large-group worship and small-group discipleship. Each group becomes a vital part of the church's mission to make disciples who know God, grow together, and live on mission in the world (Matthew 28:18–20).

Small groups are not add-ons to the church's ministry; they are essential environments where transformation happens. As Paul reminded the Thessalonians, discipleship flourishes in life-on-life relationships marked by both truth and love:

---

[184] See Shepherd, *The Barnabas Factor.*

"So, being affectionately desirous of you, we were ready to share with you not only the gospel of God but also our own selves, because you had become very dear to us" (1 Thess. 2:8, ESV).

A Call to Persevere

Leading a small group is both rewarding and challenging. There will be seasons of visible fruitfulness and times of hidden labor. There will be weeks when attendance is strong and others when discouragement tempts you to quit.

The call is not to chase success in worldly terms but to pursue faithfulness in Christ's terms. Leaders who persevere, anchored in Scripture and dependent on the Spirit, will see lives transformed. And even when results seem invisible, God is at work in ways far beyond what you can see (Isaiah 55:11).

Faithful leadership in small groups leaves a legacy of discipleship that outlasts one meeting, one group, or even one generation. The seeds sown in living rooms today may bear fruit in nations tomorrow.

Final Exhortation

So press on. Serve with humility. Shepherd with love. Multiply with courage. Remember that your labor in the Lord is never in vain (1 Corinthians 15:58). For in due season, you will reap a harvest for the glory of God and the good of His church. And when the Chief Shepherd appears, *"you will receive the unfading crown of glory"* (1 Peter 5:4, ESV).

Small group leaders are frontline disciple-makers. By God's grace, your faithfulness in the small circle of a group contributes to the great circle of God's global mission. Lead with confidence, because He who called you is faithful and He will surely do it (1 Thessalonians 5:24).

Bibliography

Arnold, Jeffrey. *The Big Book on Small Groups*. Rev. ed. Downers Grove, IL: InterVarsity Press, 2001.

Baxter, Richard. *The Reformed Pastor*. 1656. Reprint, Edinburgh: Banner of Truth, 1974.

Blanchard, Ken, and Phil Hodges. *The Servant Leader*. Nashville: Thomas Nelson, 2003.

Blomberg, Craig L., and Jennifer Foutz Markley. *The Cradle, the Cross, and the Crown: An Introduction to the New Testament*. 2nd ed. Nashville: B&H Academic, 2016.

Bonhoeffer, Dietrich. *Life Together*. Translated by John W. Doberstein. New York: Harper & Row, 1954.

Bounds, *E. M. Power through Prayer*. Grand Rapids: Baker Book House, 1991.

———. *The Complete Works of E. M. Bounds on Prayer*. Grand Rapids: Baker, 1990.

Bowman, Greg, and Bill Donahue. *Coaching Life-Changing Small Group Leaders: A Comprehensive Guide for Developing Leaders of Groups and Teams*. Downers Grove, IL: InterVarsity Press, 2006.

Bosch, David J. *Transforming Mission: Paradigm Shifts in Theology of Mission*. Maryknoll, NY: Orbis Books, 1991.

Breen, Mike, and Steve Cockram. *Building a Discipling Culture*. 3rd ed. Pawleys Island, SC: 3DM Publishing, 2017.

Braddy, Ken. *Breathing Life into Sunday School: 12 Essentials for Effective Bible Teaching*. Nashville: B&H Publishing, 2019.

————. "Four Qualities to Look for in Group Leaders." Ken Braddy: Sunday School Revolutionary, July 16, 2019. https://kenbraddy.com/2019/07/16/four-qualities-to-look-for-in-group-leaders/.

————. "Groups on Mission: Why Small Groups Must Live Sent." Ken Braddy Blog. Lifeway. Accessed September 27, 2025. https://kenbraddy.com.

————. "Handling Conflict in Your Group." Ken Braddy Blog. Lifeway. Accessed September 27, 2025. https://kenbraddy.com.

————. "Pastoral Care in Small Groups." Ken Braddy Blog. Lifeway. Accessed September 27, 2025. https://kenbraddy.com.

————. "Six Keys to Organizing and Leading Sunday School Classes and Groups." Lifeway Research Blog, April 15, 2020. https://kenbraddy.com.

————. "Why Multiplication Matters in Groups." Ken Braddy Blog. Lifeway. Accessed September 27, 2025. https://kenbraddy.com.

————. "Why Prayer Must Be Central in Your Group." Ken Braddy Blog, May 14, 2020. https://kenbraddy.com/2020/05/14/why-prayer-must-be-central-in-your-group/.

Butterfield, Rosaria. *The Gospel Comes with a House Key: Practicing Radically Ordinary Hospitality in Our Post-Christian World*. Wheaton, IL: Crossway, 2018.

Carson, D. A. *A Call to Spiritual Reformation: Priorities from Paul and His Prayers*. Grand Rapids: Baker Academic, 1992.

Carson, D. A., and G. K. Beale, eds. *Commentary on the New Testament Use of the Old Testament*. Grand Rapids: Baker Academic, 2007.

Chambers, Oswald. *My Utmost for His Highest*. Grand Rapids: Discovery House, 1992.

Christian History Institute. "The One Hundred Year Prayer Meeting." Accessed August 21, 2025. https://christianhistoryinstitute.org/magazine/article/one-hundred-year-prayer-meeting.

Clowney, Edmund P. *The Church. Contours of Christian Theology*. Downers Grove, IL: InterVarsity Press, 1995.

Coleman, Robert E. *The Master Plan of Evangelism*. 2nd ed. Grand Rapids: Revell, 1993.

Comiskey, Joel. *How to Lead a Great Cell Group Meeting...So People Want to Come Back*. Moreno Valley, CA: CCS Publishing, 2010.

Conciliar Post. "John Wesley and Small Groups." Accessed August 21, 2025. https://conciliarpost.com/christian-traditions/methodist/john-wesley-and-small-groups/.

Crabb, Larry. *Connecting: Healing Ourselves and Our Relationships*. Nashville: Thomas Nelson, 1997.

Donahue, Bill. *Leading Life-Changing Small Groups*. 3rd ed. Grand Rapids: Zondervan, 2012.

Donahue, Bill, and Russ Robinson. *Building a Church of Small Groups: A Place Where Nobody Stands Alone*. Grand Rapids: Zondervan, 2001.

Earley, Dave, and Rod Dempsey. *Leading Healthy, Growing, Multiplying Small Groups*. Houston: Touch Outreach, 2010.

Emerson, Harrington. *Twelve Principles of Efficiency*. New York: The Engineering Magazine, 1912.

ESV Study Bible. Edited by Wayne Grudem. Wheaton, IL: Crossway, 2008.

Fee, Gordon D., and Douglas Stuart. *How to Read the Bible for All Its Worth*. 3rd ed. Grand Rapids: Zondervan, 2003.

Ferguson, Dave, and Warren Bird. *Hero Maker: Five Essential Practices for Leaders to Multiply Leaders*. Grand Rapids: Zondervan, 2018.

Flake, J. N. (Arthur). *Building a Standard Sunday School*. Nashville: Sunday School Board of the Southern Baptist Convention, 1922.

Francis, David. *The Discover Triad: Three Facets of a Dynamic Adult Class*. Nashville: LifeWay, 2012.

Geiger, Eric, and Kevin Peck. *Designed to Lead: The Church and Leadership Development*. Nashville: B&H, 2016.

Getz, Gene A. *Elders and Leaders: God's Plan for Leading the Church*. Chicago: Moody, 2003.

Gladen, Steve. *Leading Small Groups with Purpose: Everything You Need to Lead a Healthy Group*. Grand Rapids: Baker, 2012.

———. *Planning Small Groups with Purpose: A Field-Tested Guide to Design and Grow Your Ministry*. Grand Rapids: Baker, 2018.

———. *Small Groups with Purpose: How to Create Healthy Communities*. Grand Rapids: Baker, 2011.

Hendricks, Howard. *Teaching to Change Lives*. Portland: Multnomah, 1987.

Hirsch, Alan. *The Forgotten Ways: Reactivating the Missional Church*. Grand Rapids: Brazos, 2006.

Howerton, Rick. *A Different Kind of Tribe: Embracing the New Small Group Dynamic*. Nashville: Serendipity House, 2009.

Hughes, R. Kent. *Liberating Ministry from the Success Syndrome*. Wheaton, IL: Crossway, 1987.

Hull, Bill. *The Disciple-Making Pastor: Leading Others on the Journey of Faith*. Rev. ed. Grand Rapids: Baker, 2007.

Kaiser, Walter C., Jr. *The Old Testament Documents: Are They Reliable and Relevant?* Downers Grove, IL: InterVarsity Press, 2001.

Keck, Gregory C. *Counseling and Pastoral Care*. Nashville: Abingdon, 2002.

Köstenberger, Andreas J., L. Scott Kellum, and Charles L. Quarles. *The Cradle, the Cross, and the Crown: An Introduction to the New Testament*. 2nd ed. Nashville: B&H Academic, 2016.

Kreider, Larry, and Jimmy Seibert. *House to House: Growing Healthy Small Groups and House Churches in the 21st Century*. Shippensburg, PA: Destiny Image, 2000.

Longman, Tremper, III. *How to Read the Bible Book by Book: A Guided Tour*. Grand Rapids: Zondervan, 2002.

Luther, Martin. *A Simple Way to Pray*. 1522.

MacArthur, John. *Pastoral Ministry: How to Shepherd Biblically*. Nashville: Thomas Nelson, 2005.

———. *The Book on Leadership*. Nashville: Thomas Nelson, 2004.

Marshall, Colin, and Tony Payne. *The Trellis and the Vine: The Ministry Mind-Shift That Changes Everything*. Kingsford, Australia: Matthias Media, 2009.

Maxwell, John C. *The 21 Irrefutable Laws of Leadership.* 10th Anniversary ed. Nashville: Thomas Nelson, 2007.

———. *The Right to Lead: A Study in Character and Courage.* Nashville: Thomas Nelson, 2001.

Miller, J. R. *Personal Friendships of Jesus.* New York: Thomas Y. Crowell, 1897.

Moore, Ralph. *Making Disciples: Developing Lifelong Followers of Jesus.* Grand Rapids: Baker Books, 2001.

Murray, Andrew. *Humility: The Beauty of Holiness.* New Kensington, PA: Whitaker House, 1982.

Murray, David, and Tom Karel. *A Christian's Guide to Mental Illness: Answers to 30 Common Questions.* Wheaton, IL: Crossway, 2021.

North American Mission Board. Evangelism Resources. Alpharetta, GA: NAMB, 2010–. https://www.namb.net/evangelism/.

Oden, Thomas C. *Pastoral Theology: Essentials of Ministry.* New York: HarperCollins, 1983.

Ogden, Greg. *Transforming Discipleship: Making Disciples a Few at a Time.* Rev. ed. Downers Grove, IL: InterVarsity Press, 2016.

Osborne, Grant R. Revelation. Baker *Exegetical Commentary on the New Testament.* Grand Rapids: Baker Academic, 2002.

Osborne, Larry. *Sticky Church*. Grand Rapids: Zondervan, 2008.

Ott, Craig, and Gene Wilson. *Global Church Planting: Biblical Principles and Best Practices for Multiplication*. Grand Rapids: Baker Academic, 2011.

Peterson, Eugene H. *The Contemplative Pastor: Returning to the Art of Spiritual Direction*. Grand Rapids: Eerdmans, 1989.

Piper, John. Brothers, *We Are Not Professionals: A Plea to Pastors for Radical Ministry*. Rev. ed. Nashville: B&H, 2013.

————. *Let the Nations Be Glad! The Supremacy of God in Missions*. 3rd ed. Grand Rapids: Baker Academic, 2010.

Poirier, Alfred. *The Peacemaking Pastor: A Biblical Guide to Resolving Church Conflict*. Grand Rapids: Baker Books, 2006.

Polhill, John B. *Acts*. Vol. 26 of The New American Commentary. Nashville: Broadman, 1992.

Purves, Andrew. *Pastoral Theology in the Classical Tradition*. Louisville: Westminster John Knox, 2001.

Putman, Jim. *Real-Life Discipleship: Building Churches That Make Disciples*. Colorado Springs: NavPress, 2010.

Putman, Jim, Bobby Harrington, and Robert E. Coleman. *DiscipleShift: Five Steps That Help Your Church to Make Disciples Who Make Disciples*. Grand Rapids: Zondervan, 2013.

Rose, Keith. "Accountability in the Bible: Relational and Redemptive." Bible.org. Accessed August 23, 2025. https://bible.org/article/accountability-bible-relational-and-redemptive.

Ryle, J. C. *A Call to Prayer*. London: William Hunt, 1878.

Sande, Ken. *The Peacemaker: A Biblical Guide to Resolving Personal Conflict*. Grand Rapids: Baker Books, 2004.

Sanders, J. Oswald. *Spiritual Leadership*. Rev. ed. Chicago: Moody, 1994.

Scazzero, Peter. *Emotionally Healthy Spirituality: It's Impossible to Be Spiritually Mature, While Remaining Emotionally Immature*. Nashville: Thomas Nelson, 2017.

————. *The Emotionally Healthy Leader: How Transforming Your Inner Life Will Deeply Transform Your Church, Team, and the World*. Grand Rapids: Zondervan, 2015.

Schreiner, Thomas R. *Paul, Apostle of God's Glory in Christ: A Pauline Theology*. Downers Grove, IL: InterVarsity Press, 2001.

Shelley, Marshall. *Well-Intentioned Dragons: Ministering to Problem People in the Church*. Minneapolis: Bethany House, 1994.

Shelton, Spence. "Preparing Leaders for Missional Small Groups." Journal of Discipleship and Family Ministry 2, no. 2 (2012): 24–37.

Shepherd, Kent. *The Barnabas Factor: A Guide to Discipleship Leadership*. Steens, MS: Shepherd Ministry Resources, 2025.

Smith, Steve, with Ying Kai. *T4T: A Discipleship Re-Revolution*. Monument, CO: WIGTake Resources, 2011.

Sobels, Ben, and Francis Chan. "The Rhythms of Discipleship." Discipleship Journal 24, no. 3 (2010): 14–19.

Spurgeon, Charles H. *Spurgeon on Prayer & Spiritual Warfare*. New Kensington, PA: Whitaker House, 1997.

———. *Twelve Sermons on Prayer*. Pasadena, TX: Pilgrim Publications, 1971.

Stanley, Andy, and Bill Willits. *Creating Community: Five Keys to Building a Small Group Culture*. Colorado Springs: Multnomah, 2004.

———. *Creating Community: Five Keys to Building a Small Group Culture*. Rev. ed. Grand Rapids: Zondervan, 2021.

Stetzer, Ed, and Eric Geiger. *Transformational Groups: Creating a New Scorecard for Groups*. Nashville: B&H, 2014.

Timmis, Steve, and Tim Chester. *Total Church: A Radical Reshaping around Gospel and Community*. Wheaton, IL: Crossway, 2008.

Towns, Elmer L. *How to Build a Successful Sunday School. Nashville*: Thomas Nelson, 1982.

———. *How to Pray: What the Bible Teaches about Genuine, Effective Prayer*. Ventura, CA: Regal, 2006.

———. *What Every Sunday School Teacher Should Know*. Grand Rapids: Baker, 2001.

Tozer, A. W. *The Knowledge of the Holy*. New York: Harper & Row, 1961.

Van Yperen, Jim. *Making Peace: A Guide to Overcoming Church Conflict*. Chicago: Moody Publishers, 2002.

Wegner, Rob, and Brian Phipps. *Find Your Place: Locating Your Calling Through Your Gifts, Passions, and Story*. Grand Rapids: Zondervan, 2019.

Willard, Dallas. *The Spirit of the Disciplines: Understanding How God Changes Lives*. San Francisco: Harper & Row, 1988.

Wright, Christopher J. H. *The Mission of God: Unlocking the Bible's Grand Narrative*. Downers Grove, IL: IVP Academic, 2006.

Appendices

Appendix 1

Sample Group Covenant

A reproducible covenant outlining commitments to confidentiality, prayer, participation, accountability, and mission. Includes signature lines for leader and members.

Our Commitment as a Group

As members of this small group, we desire to live out the biblical vision of discipleship in community (Acts 2:42–47; Heb. 10:24–25). Together, we commit to:

Confidentiality: We will guard one another's trust. What is shared in the group stays in the group (Prov. 11:13).

Participation: We will come prepared, listen well, and contribute with humility so that everyone has a voice (Phil. 2:3–4).

Prayer: We will pray for one another regularly, both in our gatherings and throughout the week (Acts 4:24; Jas. 5:16).

Accountability: We will encourage one another toward obedience to God's Word, speaking the truth in love (Eph. 4:15; Heb. 10:24).

Mission: We will look outward together, serving others and sharing Christ in word and deed (Matt. 28:19–20; John 13:35).

Signatures

Leader: _____ Date: _____

Members: _____ Date: _____

Appendix 2

Group Health Diagnostic Tool

A simple assessment worksheet with categories (Scripture, Prayer, Community, Mission, Leadership) and check boxes (✔ Often / ~ Sometimes / ✘ Rarely). Helps groups evaluate strengths and growth areas.

Instructions: Mark each statement as ✔ (Often), ~ (Sometimes), or ✘ (Rarely/Never).

Group Health Diagnostic

Category	Statements	✔ / ~ / ✘
Scripture	Our group consistently centers on	
Prayer	We spend meaningful time in	
Community	Members share life outside the	
Mission	We actively invite and serve	
Leadership	An apprentice is being equipped	

Reflection: Which area needs strengthening most? What next step will we take?

Appendix 3

Leader Development Pathway Worksheet

Stage: Participant → Apprentice → Co-Leader → Leader → Multiplier

Stage	Key Practices	Next Step
Participant	Attends faithfully, engages in discussion, begins to live out Scripture.	Identify spiritual gifts and demonstrate CORE traits (Character, Obedient, Reliable, Equippable).
Apprentice	Learns from leader; takes small responsibilities (prayer, hospitality, follow-up). Practices obedience and reliability.	Lead a segment of group time with coaching.
Co-Leader	Shares leadership duties regularly (discussion facilitation, pastoral care, outreach). Demonstrates equippability.	Facilitate an entire session with feedback.
Leader	Shepherds a group faithfully; models character and care. Begins equipping others as apprentices.	Start apprenticing another future leader.
Multiplier	Trains and releases new leaders; oversees and encourages multiplication of groups.	Launch a new group or apprentice leader into leadership.

Appendix 4

Conflict Scenarios with Solutions

Sample case studies of group conflict (dominating members, doctrinal disagreements, confidentiality issues), each with practical, biblical solutions.

1. Scenario: Two members dominate discussion, silencing others.

   Solution: Affirm their passion, then redirect: "Thanks for sharing, let's hear from someone who hasn't spoken yet."

2. Scenario: A disagreement over doctrine arises.

   Solution: Return to Scripture, affirm unity in Christ, and if unresolved, schedule follow-up with leadership.

3. Scenario: Confidential information is shared outside the group.

   Solution: Revisit covenant, meet privately with offender, and restore trust with grace and truth.

Appendix 5

Quarterly Group Calendar Template

A fill-in table for 12 weeks including columns for Scripture/Topic, Fellowship Event, Service/Outreach, and Notes.

Quarter: _____

Week	Scripture/ Topic	Fellowship Event	Service/ Outreach	Notes
1				
2				
3				
4				
5				
6				
7				
8				
9				
10				
11				
12				

Appendix 6

Prayer Walking Guide

What if My Class Has Limitations?

Whether you teach small children or your class has physical limitations, there are still ways to engage in prayer walking without physically walking. Consider the following options:

• **Map Prayer Walk:** Use a physical map or a Google map of a neighborhood or community and pray over the people who live and work there. Ask the Lord to open doors for the Gospel, bless schools, businesses, elected officials, and lift up families by name where possible. (1 Timothy 2:1-2, Matthew 9:37-38)

• **Bless Every Home App:** This free app provides tools to help you pray for your neighbors by name and build relationships with them. You can track your progress, receive daily prayer prompts, and stay intentional in interceding for your community. Visit www.blesseveryhome.com to get started. (Luke 10:2, Acts 1:8)

• **Prayer Drives:** Instead of walking, drive through neighborhoods or key locations while praying over the homes, schools, businesses, and churches. Use the same guidelines as a traditional prayer walk, praying for God's presence, protection, and salvation over the area. (Jeremiah 29:7, Ephesians 6:18)

What to Do Before a Prayer Walk?

1. Prepare Your Team – Set a time, date, location, and method (walking, mapping, driving) for your prayer walk. Ensure everyone knows the plan and purpose. (*Proverbs 16:3*)

2. Prepare Your Hearts – Pray before the prayer walk, asking God for wisdom, discernment, and opportunities to minister. Consider praying through Scripture together. A helpful resource for this is *Praying the Bible* by Donald S. Whitney. Another tool is the *5 Psalms* app, which provides daily structured prayers through the Psalms. (Psalm 119:18, Colossians 4:2)

What to Do During a Prayer Walk?

3 Tips for Prayer Walking:

1. Be Observant – Pay attention to your surroundings and let them guide your prayers. For example, seeing children's toys in a yard may prompt you to pray for the family's spiritual growth and protection. (Philippians 2:4, Colossians 1:9-10)

2. Be Obedient – Be open to divine appointments. If an opportunity arises to pray with someone, encourage them, or share the Gospel, follow the Holy Spirit's leading. (Acts 8:29-31, 2 Timothy 4:2)

3. Be Ongoing – Prayer walking should not be a one-time activity but a continual spiritual practice. Regularly commit to praying over your community. (1 Thessalonians 5:17, Galatians 6:9)

What to Do After a Prayer Walk?

1. Reflect – Gather as a group to share observations, experiences, and ways you saw God at work. Did you have an opportunity to talk with someone, pray over a need, or share the Gospel? Close this time with prayer. (Psalm 143:8, Philippians 4:6-7)

2. Repeat – Schedule another prayer walk. Consistent prayer for your community can make a lasting spiritual impact. (Luke 18:1, James 5:16)

By committing to intentional, ongoing prayer, we actively seek God's kingdom to come and His will to be done in our neighborhoods and beyond. (Matthew 6:9-10)

About The Author

Kent Shepherd has faithfully served in pastoral ministry for over two decades in both Mississippi and Louisiana. He is a graduate of Blue Mountain Christian University and earned his Master of Divinity from New Orleans Baptist Theological Seminary. Kent is currently pursuing a Doctor of Ministry at Southeastern Baptist Theological Seminary, focusing on leadership, discipleship, and church health.

Throughout his ministry, Kent has been deeply passionate about making disciples, equipping leaders, and sharing the gospel with unreached people. He is committed to building a disciple-making culture that is biblical, practical, and reproducible in any ministry context.

In addition to his pastoral work, Kent is author and workshop leader, writing books and Bible studies that equip churches, small groups, and leaders to grow spiritually and multiply disciples. His resources are designed to be both accessible and deeply rooted in Scripture, making them useful for everyday believers and ministry leaders alike.

Kent and his wife, Kristen, are blessed with two sons. Together, they are dedicated to serving Christ and advancing His kingdom.

Explore more of Kent's books and Bible studies at his Amazon Author Page: amazon.com/author/kshepherd.